To Jordan
We will miss you
Ken

Inwood Indiana

Inwood Indiana

Esther
Second Edition
Inwood Indiana Press
www.InwoodIndiana.com
Mishawaka, IN
©2010 Inwood Indiana; Glenn Lyvers
Design and editing by Glenn Lyvers.
Printed in the U.S.A.
Inwood Indiana Volume 1. Ed. 2

All rights reserved. No part of this book may be reprinted or reproduced or utilized in any form or by any electronic, mechanical, or other means, now known or hereafter invented, including photocopying or recording, or in any information or retrieval system, without express written permission of the publisher.

Contents

*All characters appearing in this work are fictitious.
Any resemblance to real persons, living or dead, is purely coincidental.*

Fiction

2	Times up	*Terry Davis*
14	Esther ***	*Glenn Lyvers*
16	Caverns of the Mind	*Bob Strother*
21	Hungry	*Bob Strother*
34	Customers	*Zdravka Vtimova*
38	Mucca	*Karen Beatty*
44	A Palm Reading	*K. Bond*
49	In God's Country	*Joseph Grant*
63	Blessed Garden	*Esther Poyer*
65	Up at the Plate	*Thomas Healy*
71	The Dead Dance All Winter Long	*Garrett Ashley*
84	Scarecrow Fort	*Ron D'alena*
88	Thicker Than Water	*Eric J. Juneau*
108	Tree Fort ***	*Darrell Carmean*
111	Peoria, Il.	Neila Mezynski

Contents

Poetry

Amy David
115   This Barn

Richard Fein
117   Dead Wires
118   My Blackmail Note to All of You
120   Possible Parallel Other
121   A Glutton for Truth
122   This Statement Is False
123   A Guilt-Free Sorry

Derek Richards
124   Annual Autumn Exodus
125   Directions on How to Ruin a Town
      How God Spoke Through Bradley
127   Fort Gloucester
128   With Apologies to the Girl behind the Counter
130   Riddance to Riddles

George Moore
131   Common Sounds
132   The Santé Fe Trail
134   The Place

Howie Good
135   One Night Stay

Johnmac the bard
136   Inwood Park
137   The Bars
139   The Friday Night Dance
140   1958

Lynda Nash
141　The Journey to Me
142　In Transit
143　On His Own Path
144　Unexpected Guests

Mary Marie Dixon
145　St. Deroin
146　Spirits of Chickens
148　House

Michael Lee Johnson
150　Gingerbread Lady
151　Harvest Time
152　Charlie Plays a Tune
153　Nikki Purrs
154　Rod Stroked Survival with a Deadly Hammer
155　Mother Edith at 98

Mike Berger
156　The Big Event
158　A Dream Come True
159　The Apotheosis of Ugly
161　Progress

Phillip A. Ellis
162　"On a Magpie"
163　"No Regrets"
164　"On a News Report"
165　"After Night-Rain"
166　"A Memory of the Old Farm"

Robert Lietz
167　Local Enterprise
169　Learning To Speak Her Own Name Twice
173　Breughel Afterward
175　Wheels

Contents

Rod Walker
177 Legacy
178 Opaque
179 Search

Tom Sheehan
180 Hawk Watch at Pranker's Pond
182 Saugus, Embassy of the Second Muse

William Hicks
185 "Land Shark!"
186 I'm Okay
189 Beeeep

Esther

Time's Up   Terry Davis

> *The local liquor store was just five doors down from his watch repair shop. 167 steps, to be precise. He had made the run frequently over the years. But this time was different. Solomon knew he was going to die the day after his seventieth birthday, which was tomorrow. So he had two days to go. The fifth of Jack Daniels was inconspicuous, he thought, in a brown paper bag, as he calmly walked along the back alleyway behind all the stores lined up in this little enclave in Bloomfield Heights, Michigan.*

It was a big deal to turn seventy. Sixty was bad enough. But now seventy, plus the information he had about his deathday.

As he stashed the whiskey away in his desk in the back office, he looked up at the portrait of his dad, Isaac Cohen, the founder of this business. Now there was a *real* craftsman. There was no broken watch or clock he couldn't repair. He knew their insides like the back of his hand. And he had built a solid clientele. The business was a monument to the concept of time. Keeping track of time was crucial; a great timepiece was an heirloom, worthy of celebration and preservation.

But since young Solomon had taken over, the business had broken down to replacing batteries in store-bought watches, mostly made in China. The watches looked good and worked well, but the battery only lasted for a year or two. When it died, Solomon could put in a new battery and have you on your way for $10.00. Not quite the same level of professional satisfaction as his dad had, but it was a living, and these days, that counted for something.

"Hi Ben." Sol said as the bells on the doorknob tinkled. Ben Grossman was a steady customer who had a collection of 50 watches, whose batteries would wind down and need replacement.

"Hi Sol. What's up?"

"Not much, same ol' same ol'"

"Got one for you. Stopped yesterday in the middle of the afternoon- right on my wrist."

"There's no predicting."

"You'd think as many watches as I have there would be a steady rhythm to the batteries dying. But they seem to come in bunches."

"Always the way. Maybe I'll teach you how to do this sometime. But right now it's job security"

"Once you retire like me, you'll settle into living within your fixed income, and job security becomes less important."

Within minutes, the back of the watch was off, a new battery replaced the old one, and the back was snapped back on. Solomon collected the money and put it into the cash register. "See you next time, Ben."

"Next time."

Solomon loved to think about time. Time was his business, but it was also a hobby for him, since he really had no others. He had concluded that time was a force that differed from other physical metrics. Mass, energy, and distance exist in three dimensional space. But underlying all of this is a fourth dimension: time. It seemed self-defining, and enormously fascinating. The problem was that all definitions of time were circular: referred back to themselves. What is a minute?: 60 seconds. What is a second? One sixtieth of a minute; etc.

He even dreamed about time. So it wasn't a surprise in 2004 when he had a dream he will never forget. In the dream, his only brother, Tom, five years his junior, and a Psychiatrist in Los Angeles, had told him the exact day he was going to die: August 23th, 2009. No other details, just the date. It was quite bizarre, because immediately after Tom named the date, he turned into a miniature globe which progressively diminished in size until all was black. Solomon woke up, drenched in sweat, turned on the light, and grabbed the spiral notebook on his bedside table in which he kept all of his lists and journal entries, along with the number 2 lead pencil which he always kept sharpened along side, and wrote down the date of his death from the dream: August 23, 2009. That would be just one day after his seventieth birthday. But he immediately dismissed the information as not reliable, part of a strange dream, and forgot about it.

The problem is that the exact same date came up again two years later. Solomon lived in an apartment complex on the outskirts of Bloomfield Hills. A lifelong bachelor with no children or immediate family, he had lots of time to kill when he wasn't at the shop. He worried about how much time he spent on the internet, to the point he had a stop watch by the computer, and set it for 2 hours when he sat down each night. A ten minute and a five minute warning programmed in the timer gave him time to log off and shut down, beginning his pre-bedtime check list, including his night time toiletry routine, a double check of the lock and the dead bolt on his apartment door, and setting the coffee to brew at 6:30AM the next day.

So the day his acquaintance, Barney Mansfield, who owned the art gallery complex two stores down from him told him about this particular web site, he had to break his regular internet routine. Solomon and Barney were chatting one evening in the walkway behind the stores. Barney said that a number of the co-op artists at his gallery, as well as one of the customers, had been talking about this website called "Deathday.com". You enter information about yourself: birth date, information about parents, how old they were when they died, what they died of, smoking history, and other health information. The website then tells you the exact date you will die. Of course there are lots of disclaimers about being only for entertainment. But on several occasions recently, reportedly, people had actually died on the date the website predicted.

That evening, after he closed the store, he went home and set his internet timer. But before he started, he poured an extra shot of Jack Daniels into his normal nightcap, and logged onto www.deathday.com. It took him a full 30 minutes to put in all the information. For normal people it wouldn't take that much time, but Solomon had to put in everything exactly correctly, full dates of parental deaths, exact dosages of all medications he took including his over-the-counter vitamins, and so forth. He hesitated for a moment, poured himself an unprecedented refill on his Jack Daniels, and then pushed "enter". Up it came on the screen, in black letters, filling up the box: August 23, 2009. Solomon immediately went to the top right shelf over his desk where he keeps his old spiral notebooks, and went to the one from two years prior. He paged back through to the time he remembered that dream, and there it was. The same date! Although he had dismissed the date the first time, it seemed too weird for the exact same date to come up twice- two years apart, from two different sources. So slowly over the next two weeks, it gained the status of a fact in his mind.

The first visible evidence of this acceptance was his journal, into which he put an entry every day, whether or not he had something to say. For over a decade he had started each day's entry with not only the date, but the day of his life, "DOL": how many days he had been alive.

"June 22, 2006---DOL 24,381. Strange thing happened today. I looked up on the Internet the day I am going to die, and it came up with the same date I wrote down after my dream two years ago. . . the exact same date! What are the odds?"

One week later, his degree of acceptance of the information as fact (even though he told himself it was "entertainment value only") was evident in the new format for his journal entry.

"June 29, 2006---DOL 24,388/25,568. Knowing the denominator sure changes things around. At first I thought it would be upsetting, but now that I know my deathday, it's kind of liberating. I know I'm not going to die today, so I can take some chances. I'll have to think of what stuff I could do, knowing that I don't have to worry."

He approached the information about his deathday the way he approached everything else in his life: deliberately, methodically, and unemotionally. As he entered his last year, not much changed. His afternoon nip of Jack Daniels in his back office during the afternoon slump doubled to two shots, but otherwise the routine remained the same. His finances had already been in order, so there was nothing to clean up. His checkbook had always been balanced to the penny each week. He had no one relying on him in any way, so there was nobody who had to be prepared for his departure. He had decided to tell no one at all, and was prepared just to let whatever was going to happen, happen.

As he moved into his final sixty days, he had concluded that at least it was not going to be a long lingering chronic painful illness that would take him, because he would have known that by now. That was a relief.

The only unresolved and increasingly troubling issue in his mind was what to do about the business. Every day he would look up at the portrait of his father over the desk and think about all the decades that had gone into making the business what it is now. Some days he thought it would just let it go. A once honorable trade had degenerated into simply swapping out batteries. No big deal. Let the probate court decide. But other days he would realize how much of his self image was tied up in this shop, and how it was a good, steady living at this time when unemployment in Michigan had gone up to 11%. He should will it to someone. But to whom? His younger brother, Tom, lived in California, and was busy with his psychiatric practice, a young wife, and two young kids. He would have no interest. Solomon had no close friends in town. He had never fallen in love with anyone; certainly not with any woman. A couple of brief relationships with men in his 20s and 30s had left him confused and isolated. He had never come to grips with any of that. The more he thought about who should get the business, the more he realized how lonely and unattached he was.

> *"July 9, 2009---DOL 25,524/25,568 44 days left and I can't figure out what to do with the business. Today I tried to make a list of friends or family that might like to take it over. I came up with no one. For over an hour I stared at the number 1. Nothing. This sucks."*

"Hi Ben." Solomon said as the door opened to produce the first customer of the day. Ben had arrived with a little sack of three wrist watches.

"Hi Sol. What's up?"

"Not much. Same ol' same ol'"

"Three this time. Don't know why I keep all these watches going. No need to keep track of time anymore."

"Maybe I <u>should</u> teach you this trade. You could help out here in the shop for fun."

"I'll have to think about that."

> *"July 5, 2009---DOL 24,394/25/568. I could will the business to Ben Grossman. He is retired from the banking business, and he loves watches. If he inherited the shop, he could either learn how to do the trade, or hire someone to do it. I'll change my will tomorrow. No need for him to know anything about it.*

The phone rang. "Hello?"

"Hi Sol. Tom here"

"Tom! How the hell are you? It been a long time." In fact, they hadn't seen each other since their mother's funeral six years ago. When she died, they were the only two left of the family.

"It <u>has</u> been a while. I'm good. How about you?"

"Same ol', same ol'. Business is holding up in spite of the recession. Actually up a bit. People are holding on to their old watches more. Buying fewer new ones. How's Monica and the kids?"

"Fine. She's full time stay-at-home. The twins are being two year olds. I forgot how much energy they have. It's a lot for a 65 year old to keep up with."

"Yeah, but you're up to it."

"Sol, the reason I called is that our Society meets in Detroit this year toward the end of August. I'm giving a paper at the meetings, so I need to come. It's around your 70th birthday, so I thought I could take you out to dinner to celebrate on the 22nd."

"Psychiatrists meeting in Detroit? Couldn't you find a more . . . exotic city?"

"With all the University travel restrictions, Detroit made sense. You on?"

"Sounds great. I'll free up the evening." Solomon said, knowing he had nothing else on his docket.

"Great. See you then."

Love to Monica and the kids"

"Backatcha" Tom barked into the phone as he hung up.

> *"August 1, 2009 - - - DOL 25,546/25,568. Tom called today. He's coming out to talk at a meeting of the national Psychiatric Society, and asked me out to dinner for my birthday. That'll be nice, but a little strange. What will we talk about? We've never been close. My fault? I can't tell him what I know. He'd slap some psychiatric diagnosis on me- commit me to a place where they would keep me on a suicide watch"*

They met at the Tribute Restaurant in Farmingdale on Friday night, August 22, 2009, Solomon's 70th birthday, and the day before his Deathday. The concierge at Tom's hotel had recommended it as the best in the Detroit area. Hot and steamy weather had settled into the Midwest. A line of severe thunderstorms had moved in around 4PM and the tornado watch accompanying them had just expired. Solomon had dressed up for the occasion with a blue blazer, tan slacks, a blue business shirt, and his dark blue tie covered with dozens of different kinds of watches that Ben Grossman had given him for his birthday two years earlier.

He recognized Tom immediately, who had apparently come directly from the meetings, wearing his charcoal grey, pin striped suit, white shirt and red tie. He had neglected to take off his lanyard name tag draped around his neck.

"You must be Tom Cohen." Sol joked as he pointed to the name tag. Tom, embarrassed, immediately took it off and put it in his jacket pocket.

"I'll have a Beefeaters Martini. Straight up. With a twist." Ben announced to the server.

Encouraged by that, Solomon said "Jack Daniels on the rocks. Water on the side."

The conversation started out easily enough. It took roughly twenty minutes and most of the first drink for Tom to fill Sol in on Monica's loving to be a mom, and the twins, and their milestones, and how different they are, and being a new dad as an older man.

"So what's up with you, old man? Imagine: 70 years old."

"Not much. Same ol' same ol'" he said with full assurance that tomorrow was his deathday. "Just workin' Dad's shop- trying to figure out who I can hand it off to."

"Hand it off? You're still young. Got lots of time."

As he started into his second drink, Solomon recognized he was sitting across the table from his only living relative. All these years, neither of them had really made any effort to get to know one another. Most of Solomon's life had been dull and predictable. Actually even knowing his deathday seemed a fitting end to a perfectly predictable life. Yet it also seemed rather remarkable. He came with inches of telling his story to Tom, but never could cross the line.

"So tell me about the paper you presented today." Thus the conversation shifted away from Solomon and never returned for the rest of the evening. Dinner ended with an empty hug including mutual loud claps on the back and an agreement not to let so much time go by before they get back together again. For a brief moment Solomon thought he had one last chance to say something, but didn't.

"August 22, 2009 ---DOL 25,567/25,568. Tom and I had dinner tonight for my birthday. It was nice. I thought about telling him about what I know, but didn't. He's pretty much wrapped up in his own life right now. It would be nice to have somebody to talk to. I am going to double up on the sleeping pills tonight so at least I can get some sleep. I don't know why I care, but I don't want to sit up all night thinking about it. Two weeks ago when I got the pills from Dr. Nease after telling him I was having trouble sleeping, I thought about just taking the whole bottle, and not having to go through whatever is coming tomorrow. But then I figured it wouldn't work, because it wasn't my deathday yet. I would just end up embarrassed in some hospital. And even if it did work, I have always thought people who commit suicide are kind of cowards, and I wouldn't want my life to end that way."

The alarm went off as usual at 6:30AM. The higher dose of sleeping pills had worked so the alarm jolted him awake. As he moved into consciousness he immediately noticed an unfamiliar sensation: anxiety. In his obsessive compulsive way, to this point he had been able to successfully compartmentalize his feelings about today, so that he really never thought about it, only the preparations for it. Now here it was: his deathday. What was going to happen? How would it feel? Would there be pain? Or would it just be . . . lights out? What's next? He couldn't put those questions off anymore, and the more he thought about them, the more scared he became.

So he planned to just dive into his routine. By 8:00AM he arrived at his store after a very meager breakfast- he wasn't hungry. As he got out of his car at the strip mall, the intensely muggy air made him decide to lower the thermostat in the shop despite the extra cost that would tack onto the electric bill. *"What the hell. What do I care?"* He opened the front door and turned the sign around so that it read "Open-Come In" from the street instead of "Sorry, We're Closed". He went to the back office and looked at the picture of his father, wondering what his dad would do in this situation. He turned the morning news on the TV in the back office.

One idea he had was that he might die in a major terrorist attack. Detroit could be a target, but Bloomfield Hills is far enough from Detroit that it would have to be a major nuclear bomb. Such an attack would likely be timed for maximum effect around rush hour, so as 9:00AM moved on to 10:00AM that possibility seemed to go away. Actually, Solomon had figured out that being vaporized by a nuke would be a "lights out" scenario, which he had begun to hope for.

The door bells jingled. It was Ben Grossman.

"Hi Ben."

"Hi Sol. What's up?"

"Same ol' same ol'. You?"

As Ben put his watch onto the counter, Solomon motioned for Ben to come around to the table where he does his work. "OK. It's time. Let me show you how it's done." He put on his magnifying glasses and with one swift twist of a miniature screw driver, he had the back off and was looking down at a tiny circular battery with a "+" on its back. He took it out and looked at the front. "It's a 3414" he said as he tossed the old battery into a fish bowl containing many hundred spent batteries of all different sizes. The jar must have weighed ten or fifteen pounds. Once every couple of years, Solomon had emptied it and sent the batteries off to a recycler. He pulled out one of the dozens of little drawers on the edge of the table- the one labeled "3414", un-wrapped a fresh battery, and put it in. Then he placed the watch face down on the press, positioned the back squarely in place, and squeezed the lever which popped the back in.

"There you go" Solomon said as he set the watch to the proper time. "Now you know how to do it. Next time, you can try."

"I'll do that. It'll be fun."

Fortunately it was busy for a Saturday, but Solomon got more and more jumpy as the day went on. Several commercial airliners on their approach to Detroit International seemed somewhat low and he thought they may be landing short right in his store, but none did.

Late in the afternoon he watched the Weather Channel on his TV in the back office, and they were warning about yet another line of severe thunderstorms that was approaching Bloomfield Hills. They were issuing a tornado watch. As it got darker outside the store, he went outside to see the sky. Stepping out from his air conditioned store to the sidewalk felt like walking into a steam bath. The skies were dark and foreboding. He felt his heart pounding even before the tornado siren started wailing. *"No sense seeking shelter"* he thought to himself as the street lights went on in response to the darkness. Then he heard the sound he had always heard described: like a freight train, coming ever closer. Incredibly loud noise came as ear popping pressure changes and a huge rush of wind forced Solomon back inside his store. "This is it" he thought, as he closed his eyes and waited for "it" to happen. His heart was pounding. He just wanted it to be over. But as quickly as it started, it was over. He was still alive. The sky brightened, and the sun came out. Then the sirens began from the police, ambulances, and fire trucks. The tornado had touched down only a block away, and had cut a swath of destruction ¼ mile wide and two miles long, just barely missing Solomon's store. Soon the thump-thump-thump of the news helicopters dominated the soundscape as they converged on the scene to cover the story. Several people had been killed, rescue operations were proceeding. He watched it numbly on the news as he closed up the store, and took one last look at his father over the desk. He turned the sign from "Open- Come In" to "Sorry-We're Closed" and locked the door.

He got into his car to drive home, and his hands were shaking as he put the key in the ignition. His normal route home was blocked by tornado damage and rescue operations, so he drove an alternate route. It seemed as if every approaching truck was about to go left of center and drive head on into him. Two different times he actually swerved over to the right, almost running other cars off the road.

When he arrived at his apartment, astounded that he had made it, he wasn't really hungry for dinner. This was Saturday and that was usually the Lean Cuisine Beef Stroganoff. But he had a couple of Jack Daniels and some cheese and crackers instead. What the hell.

After the National News, "Jeopardy" was preempted by local coverage of the tornado touchdown and the ongoing search for additional survivors with the death toll now up to 5. By the third Jack Daniels, Solomon was wondering if some glitch in the GPS of the tornado had caused it to miss its intended victim by a single block. How sad that innocent people got caught up in this whole mess.

It was 8:00PM- 5:00 in Los Angeles, Solomon thought. By now, Tom would be finished his office hours. Solomon had been thinking about this all day, if he made it this far. Tom had given Solomon his cell phone number. Solomon picked up the phone, stared for a moment at the key board, and then slowly punched in Tom's number. Three rings, and then a click. "Hi. You've reached Dr. Tom Cohen. I'm not available to take your call right now, but leave me a message, and I'll get back to you as soon as possible." Then the beep. Solomon took a long breath as he gently pressed the "disconnect" button and put the phone down.

He had so rarely cried that the sensation of welling sadness, the lump in his throat, and the uncontrollable quivering of his lips were strangers to him. Actual tears fell on his spiral notebook as he poured another Jack Daniels and entered his final note.

> *"August 23, 2009- - -DOL 27,568/27,568. I just tried to call Tom. Just wanted to talk to him one more time- not even sure what I wanted to say. But I got his answering machine. I couldn't leave a message because I was beginning to cry and I didn't want him to remember me that way. So much we could have talked about. If only I had started earlier.*
>
> *I haven't died yet. So many times it could have happened today, but it hasn't yet. The tornado that was sent to get me missed by a single block. Poor bastards got caught in the cross fire. It wasn't their fault.*
>
> *There are only 3 hours left so it looks like its going to happen in my sleep. I'll take enough pills to make sure it doesn't wake me up. Good night."*

At 6:30AM the next morning the alarm went off as usual.

Esther

When she was dull, dull and tired of watching TV or any number of mundane tasks, she would go out to the garage to investigate. The garage sat where great poplars once stood, casting their wintery skeleton-shadows upon the snow. The nobility was gone, replaced by the laughter of teenagers playing pool and cheating the pinball Gods.

Esther had filled the garage with coin operated games and a pool table. Maybe she did it because she needed the money, or maybe she wanted to attract the children—but whatever her reasons were, she did attract the children, all of them. This brought about a kind of paranoia in Esther. She would pace the floors inside her modest yellow house, glancing out the windows to the garage. She would become angry and exclaim "they better not be getting into anything out there!" These thoughts would consume her, and send her out to the garage, over and over throughout the day. Until one January day, her worst fears were realized.

Esther went out to open the garage door at 7AM only to find the door wide open. She walked inside. Something about the crisp winter air erased any idea that something was wrong. At first she thought she must have forgotten to lock up last night, but she did. She locked both of the padlocks and now she could see them in pieces scattered across the floor inside. Ester stood in the garage, looking at the broken lock on the pool table. It was a violation! Wasn't she the one who put wood in the stove? Wasn't she the one who made the change for the table to begin with? She stood there in her yellow housecoat and red slippers, with the keys to the table in one hand, and an empty purse in the other. A long moment passed before she noticed the wood axe was chipped. "I know what to do with you," she murmured. "The next kid to walk through that door is going to get it!"

For the next 30 minutes she shuffled her feet around the garage. She wondered if she should really kill the next child who came in, or if she should raise the prices and make everyone repay the loss of her $10. The cool air chipped away at her anger little by little, until at last she lit the little stove to warm the garage for the children who would certainly be arriving soon. She took the axe and turned to follow her footprints in the snow back to the yellow house.

    The chill had taken its toll. She was as old as any of the poplars, and better known. Her age and the emotional drain of the morning had taxed her severely. The stoic face of the businesswoman had slid into a defeated sadness, like a wax face melting. Her steps were shorter going back, and her feet barely lifted from the ground. She did not notice that the birds didn't stir as she passed them on her way back to the house. She looked like an old tree walking.

    Once inside, Esther leaned on the chest freezer, resting. While she stood there, her strength slowly returned until at last she felt strong enough to move again. She placed her frail hands on the chest freezer and pushed the top open. Snow-like frost fell into tiny white piles and a cool fog flowed out like little clouds thinning quickly. Esther looked at her husband's corpse inside the freezer and said, "Can you believe they would do that to me?" – she put the ax inside the freezer and closed the door.

Glenn Lyvers

Caverns of the Mind

Bob Strother

Josh's foot slipped and sent loose pebbles skittering down into the vast darkness on his left. He pressed his back against the cold stone wall above the narrow ledge and waited for his heartbeat to slow. They'd been in the cave for twenty minutes. From further up along the rock shelf, he heard Paul's reassuring voice and it calmed him. "It's only a little further. The ledge widens out up here and there's an opening."

Josh knew he would be all right as long as his friend was with him. At thirteen, a year older than Josh himself, Paul had the self-confidence of an adult—maybe even more than most adults. In the year or so since Paul came along, Josh had never seen him at a loss for how to handle any given situation.

His flashlight caught Paul's lanky body perched casually on the edge of a rock overhang. From Josh's lower angle, the beam transformed Paul's face into a mask of light and shadow. He was grinning—a toothy grin that made Josh think of a Jack-O-Lantern.

"C'mon," Paul urged. "This is really cool, isn't it?"

They'd been shooting birds with Josh's BB gun when they found the cave back in the woods behind Bronson's General Store. The entrance was almost completely hidden by a thicket of blackberry bushes heavy with summer fruit. Bagging Blue Jays had paled beside this discovery. At Josh's house, they'd filled a worn rucksack with flashlights, bottled water and snack foods, then high-tailed it back to the woods.

Josh's heart rate finally returned to normal. "Yeah," he answered, his voice little more than a whisper. "It's really cool."

"You don't have to whisper," Paul said. "We're in a cave. You can shout." He leaned back toward an irregular dark opening in the wall behind him and yelled, "Hello!" The echo reverberated through the chamber, eventually tapering off to nothingness. "You try it," Paul said.

Josh did try it. He almost always did as Paul suggested. This time the echo faded more quickly.

Or did it?

"Listen!" Paul said.

They heard it again, faintly, from somewhere deeper into the cave. "Hello!" the voice cried. "Help me! Please help me!"

Paul reached down. "Quick, give me your hand. Let's go see."

The two boys scrambled through the opening and along a wide, flat area that gradually narrowed and finally angled off into two separate passageways.

Josh called out again. "Where are you?"

"Here!" the voice shouted, closer now. It sounded female. "I'm down here."

Josh followed Paul into the tunnel on the left. It was slow going at first because the passageway was low-ceilinged and the boys had to crawl on hands and knees. After a few moments, the tunnel ended and they came to another ledge opening out into a much larger room of the cave.

Josh shined his flashlight over the edge. Jagged walls of rock sloped down twenty or more feet from the ledge to form a roughly oval-shaped floor. The shaft of light stopped on a small form huddled among the stalagmites.

"Oh God, oh thank you," the woman said. "Thank you so much!"

"C'mon," Josh said, and the boys picked their way down through the rocks to the floor of the cave.

She was in her late twenties, Josh thought, and in spite of the grime covering her face, she was very pretty. He stared at her, wanting to reach out and touch her, but of course he didn't. Instead, he handed her one of the bottles of water and she drank from it greedily. "What happened to you?" he asked.

"I was hiking—backpacking." She gestured to a yellow nylon pack leaning against one of the mineral formations. "There's a trail not far from here. The map showed a store nearby and I was on my way there when I saw some blackberry bushes." She paused, squeezed her eyes shut, and twin tears rolled slowly down her cheeks. "I stopped to pick a few."

"And you saw the cave entrance," Josh offered.

She nodded.

"And decided to explore."

Another nod.

"And you got this far and…?"

"I fell," she said in a tiny voice. "I fell from the ledge up there and hurt my leg."

Josh lowered his flashlight to the young woman's legs. They were bruised and scraped and one was badly swollen. Probably broken, he thought.

"I tried to climb back up, but then I fell again."

"How long have you been here?" Josh asked.

"I don't know. My flashlight broke and I couldn't see my watch. I ran out of food and water and I thought—" She began to cry harder and buried her face in her hands.

"Shhh," Josh said, touching his forefinger to his lips. "You'll be all right now, but we'll need help getting you out of here." He dumped the contents of the rucksack out on the ground. "In the meantime, eat this stuff and—" he handed her one of the flashlights—"hang onto to this."

He and Paul climbed carefully back up through the rocks to the ledge. Josh paused just before they entered the passageway. "What's your name?"

"Marissa," she called back. "Marissa Collins. And … please hurry!"

Josh nodded in the pale glow from her flashlight then knelt and followed Paul into the tunnel.

They emerged from the mouth of the cave nearly half an hour later. Josh blinked in the warm summer sunlight and stretched to work the kinks from his muscles. "We can go to Bronson's, I guess. That'd be the closest place."

Paul stood looking back into the cave entrance. "I guess."

Josh grinned, thinking of how cool this was going to be. They might even get their pictures in the *Inwood Messenger*. "C'mon, let's go be heroes."

Paul turned slowly and his gray-green eyes locked with Josh's. "We *could* do that—be heroes for a while. Or…"

"Or what?"

Paul stepped closer and his voice was soft, like a breeze streaming through tall pines. "Or … we could have something special, something that could last a lifetime. Can you imagine?" He slipped his arm around Josh's shoulders and they walked off through the woods.

By the time they passed Bronson's store, the thought of heroics had given way to the greatest secret *ever*.

***

The boys went back to the cave once more, on a Saturday in late October. The reason for their return—whether morbid curiosity, or something of a more transcendental nature—was never discussed.

Marissa lay in her sleeping bag, still and quiet. Snack food wrappers littered the ground around her. The flashlight, long since dead, lay clasped in one hand like an icon of hope.

"Go ahead," Paul said. "Touch her. I know you wanted to."

Josh reached out and ran trembling fingers tenderly along the side of the young woman's neck. Her skin felt cool and smooth, leathery, like his mother's handbag.

He looked over at Paul and smiled.

***

"Josh! Did you hear me? Open this door right now!"

His sister's strident cry pierced Josh's brain like a needle. He looked over at Paul, who sat cross-legged on the bed, reading a dog-eared issue of Mad Magazine.

"What now?" Josh said. "Another Complaint of the Week?"

"Don't look at me," Paul said. "She's *your* sister."

Josh sighed, pushing away from his desk. "You've got that right." He opened the door and Lisa stood framed in the entranceway, hands on her skinny hips. Her face showed a mixture of anger and contempt. She was only two years older than him, but had recently assumed the role of household enforcer.

"You know the rules, Josh. No locked doors. Mom and Dad said so."

"I only lock the door to keep *you* out—not Mom and Dad."

Lisa stepped inside the bedroom and looked around slowly. "Who were you talking to, anyway?"

Josh glanced at Paul, who simply shrugged and kept on reading. Lisa didn't see Paul. She never did.

Lisa smirked. "I think maybe you're going bonkers, you little troll. I may just have to have a talk with Mom about you. Maybe recommend you go see a shrink." She looked him up and down with disgust. "God knows *what* you do when you're in here by yourself." She slammed the door on her way out.

Paul looked up from his magazine. "That could be bad for us, you know—if you had to see a shrink?"

Josh nodded.

Paul studied the ceiling, rubbing his chin thoughtfully. "I think we should talk Lisa into taking a hike in the woods soon, talk things over, work out our problems."

Josh nodded again, grinning now. Paul was the *best*.

Paul matched Josh's grin with one of his own, his eyes dancing with amusement. "Maybe do a little caving?"

Hungry   Bob Strother

Buchard "Shard" McConnell the Third was hungry—head-hurting, gut-roiling, hands-trembling hungry. Five hours since breakfast. Didn't these backwoods hill people believe in restaurants? He took his eyes off the narrow dirt and gravel road just long enough to glance down into the trash-littered floorboard of his Dodge Colt and reach for a half-empty bag of nacho chips. The right side of the car dropped off the shoulder into a ditch and low-hanging tree branches exploded against the windshield. McConnell yanked the steering wheel hard left, trying desperately to keep the vehicle from abandoning the road entirely. Gravel pounded the Colt's metal underbody like machine gun fire, drowning out the anguished cry escaping his throat.

The whole thing was over in a flash. McConnell sat gasping for air, his chest heaving with adrenalin as gray dust hung heavy in the air around him. The car was canted right—half on, half off the road—and the seatbelt bit painfully into the soft flesh of his upper torso.

"Damn, damn, *damn*!" He struggled at opening the door, finally bracing it with his foot. Unbuckling the seatbelt, he carefully leveraged himself up and out of the car. No small feat for a guy whose weight hovered dangerously close to the big three-oh-oh mark.

The car, Shard. What about the car?

He walked first to the rear of the vehicle then picked his way across the ditch to the edge of the wooded area. The tailpipe was torn loose from its mooring and lay like a crumpled drinking straw in the road. The right front tire was flattened—*Not just the tire. Look at the way the wheel is jutting out. That's kind of an odd angle, isn't it?* – and the windshield was a spider web of cracks that extended top to bottom, left to right.

For a moment, anger overcame his hunger. "Arrrggg! You son of a bitch!" McConnell bent down, grabbed a stone the size of his fist and hurled it at the windshield. The safety glass shattered into marble-sized pellets and rained down across the dashboard and seats.

His anger satisfied, he went back to the right-side window, fished out the nacho chips and stuffed a handful into his mouth. *Couple more handfuls and that's it. This is serious.* He leaned against the Colt's fender and finished the chips, licking his forefinger to scavenge crumbs from the bottom corners of the bag, trying to decide what to do next.

He'd been on this poor excuse for a road nearly an hour and had seen nothing but dense woodlands pocked with an occasional small meadow. No buildings, no mailboxes, no sign that he was even within the boundaries of civilization. *And maybe, just maybe you're not, Shard.* The thought gave him a little tingle. Tossing the bag aside, he stepped out to the middle of the road where a narrow slice of early-afternoon sunshine afforded a touch of reassurance. On either side of the roadbed, the land sloped sharply upward. He wondered how long before the sun dropped below the mountainous terrain. It was only late October, but he could feel a cool dryness in the air. *It's colder in the mountains. Dark earlier, too.*

Shard checked his cell phone. No signal. No surprise. Walking back to the main road would take hours. Continuing in the direction he'd been traveling would be a crapshoot for sure. But a crapshoot was better than a sure no-win, wasn't it? He plucked a light cotton sweater from the back seat of the Colt, tied the sleeves over his shoulders and started walking. It was two-fifteen. He'd walk two hours out, and if nothing showed, walk two hours back to the car for the night. At first light, he could head back to the main road and call a tow truck.

An hour and twenty minutes later, he saw the sign. It was almost completely covered with kudzu vine, and as he ripped away at the leafy tentacles, he felt a surge of hope.

E. F. Love's General Store .5 miles

Then he felt a surge of fear. What if the store was closed? What if that was the reason the sign was covered with kudzu? What if no one cared anymore because the owner, sadly, had passed away back in the winter of '95? *Get hold of yourself, Shard. It's only half a mile. Maybe ten minutes of uncertainty. You can do that easy.*

McConnell's steps quickened as he started off again. Minutes later, when the edge of a weathered storefront crept into view, he began to run—an awkward, loping gait common to many who've continually failed to push back from the table. And when he spied a solitary figure sitting in a rocker on the store's front porch, he almost cried out for joy.

Seconds later, he leaned hands-first against the raised floor of the porch, struggling for breath. From above him, the man he'd seen asked, "You all right, young fella?"

McConnell nodded. "Got food?" he asked, still gasping.

"We're a general store. We generally have food." The man chuckled at his own joke. "Mavis'll help you after you catch your breath."

McConnell pushed off from the porch and stumbled up the steps and into the store. In less than a minute, he came out clutching two cellophane-wrapped honey buns and a Coca-Cola, and sat down on the edge of the steps. His fingers trembled as he tore the wrapping open and stuffed half of the first bun into his mouth. Honeyed sweetness coursed through his body and he moaned with relief.

"Always been partial to the cream horns, myself," the man said. "But I like honey buns too, heated up in the oven."

McConnell finished the first bun and drained most of his soft drink before he spoke. "Sorry—don't mean to be rude. I just haven't eaten in a while. Car ran off the road a few miles back."

"Take your time," the man said. He pulled a corncob pipe from his shirt pocket and lit it with a wooden match, the smoke drifting in swirls around his face as he rocked. "We got all afternoon. Name's Love, by the way, like the sign says."

McConnell heaved himself up off the steps and walked over to the store owner. The man was in his early fifties, clean-shaven and lean, with small, amused eyes. "Buchard McConnell the Third, but most people call me Shard." He held out a hand, then realized it was sticky with sugar and quickly wiped it on his trousers.

Love took his hand without getting up and appeared not to notice any remaining residue. "We don't get many visitors out this way, Mister McConnell, or maybe you just got lost."

"I'll let you tell me, Mister Love. I was headed for Poplar—"

"Yep, you're lost for sure. Took the wrong turn off Route Eighty. Closest settlement around here's Buladean, which ain't sayin' much." Love took another puff on the pipe then used a half-straightened paper clip to scratch around in the bowl. "Not much in Poplar, either. You have kinfolk there?"

"Oh no, sir. See, I'm a writer for *Ozarks' Trace* magazine." *C'mon now, you're a stringer—not a staff writer—and nowhere near the contributing editor you want so much to be.* "I heard there was a family of folks near Poplar that still spoke the Old English language." McConnell's heartbeat accelerated again just thinking about it. This could be "The Story"—the one that transformed him from fat struggling wannabe to highly-respected journalist. "I was hoping to find them, you know, maybe interview them, write their story—make 'em famous?"

"Well," Love said, "I wouldn't know 'bout that. Some folks don't want to be famous, I'd reckon. Like their privacy."

McConnell finished off the second honey bun. He was feeling better now, on a sugar high. "Yeah, well, if I could use your telephone—"

"Sorry, no phone."

"No phone?"

"Nope. Got no need for one." Love pushed up out of the rocker, stretched, and stepped over to the front door, motioning for McConnell to join him. He opened the door and waved McConnell in. "Take a look. What do you see?"

The store had a counter supporting an old-fashioned cash register on the left. On either side of the register stood metal racks of chips and crackers, pastries, and candy bars—the only items McConnell had noticed on his earlier entry. The woman he guessed was Love's wife sat behind the counter reading a dog-eared paperback. She smiled at him as his gaze swept past her. On the far wall in the rear of the room, sat a long, low freezer and a bright red soft-drink cooler with *Coca-Cola* emblazoned in white across its front. The remainder of the floor and wall space was filled with barrels and racks of fresh produce—pumpkins and pole beans, potatoes and squash, and a few items McConnell didn't recognize. He walked over and picked up a strange-looking lump.

"Rutabaga," Love said. "The thing is, see, folks around here are pretty self-sufficient. They grow most of what they need or trap it, shoot it, or ... otherwise make do. The store mostly just provides an outlet for the farmers to sell what they don't eat..." He pointed to the racks of snack food. "...and buy a few treats they can't grow."

McConnell nodded then shrugged. "But about the phone ..."

The woman spoke. "Get to the point, E. F. The young man doesn't have all day."

"Oh that. Well, as I was getting to—Mavis and I'll make the trip to town once a week or so and stock up on snacks and soft drinks. We're too far out and don't have the sales volume to rate a delivery truck, so ..."

"No need for a phone," McConnell said.

"Exactly."

"But you do have a truck?"

"Eighty-six Chevy—only eighteen thousand miles."

McConnell's face brightened. "So, could you—"

"Sure could," Love said, "first thing in the morning."

McConnell started to speak, but the woman cut him off.

"E. F. don't see all that well at night. Neither do I. We'd oblige you, but it'd be full dark by the time we started back."

"What about tonight? Is there someplace I can stay tonight?" McConnell asked. The sugar high was wearing off and he could feel a new gnawing in his stomach.

"Not here, I'm afraid," Love said, gesturing toward a narrow door between the counter and the rear wall. "Mavis and I have a couple of rooms at the back of the store but we couldn't accommodate a big fellow like you." He frowned and rubbed his chin. "What do you think, Mavis? The Leatherbys?"

"Oh sure," the woman said. "The Leatherbys would love some company. And they have that extra room, too, since the older boy left."

Love snapped his fingers. "It's settled then. Some paper, please."

The woman found a note pad and pencil and pushed it across the counter.

"I'm going to write you a note of introduction," Love said, "and explain your situation." He scribbled on the pad for a minute, signed with a flourish and ripped the page free of its binding. "C'mon back outside, Mister McConnell, and I'll point you in the right direction."

McConnell fell in behind the man and stopped at the edge of the porch. Love shielded his eyes against the late-afternoon sun and pointed up at a mountainside splotched with dark evergreens and a wild array of fall color.

"There," Love said.

"What? Where?"

"There," Love said again, waggling his finger. "Right about halfway to the top. See the meadow?"

McConnell squinted into the distance, finally spotting a pale yellow rectangle the size of a postage stamp nestled amid conifers in varying hues of green. "How far is that?"

"Bout half a mile, but it's a mite steep climb." Love folded the note and offered it to McConnell. "You'll probably want another soft drink for the road."

Love escorted him to a narrow strip that was little more than two wheel ruts in the dirt. McConnell waved a tentative goodbye to the store owner and started up the mountainside.

Ten minutes later, he sat down heavily on a fallen tree trunk, swallowed the last of his cherry soda, and tossed the bottle into the brush. Sweat ran from his temples and dark stains covered the front of his shirt and under his arms. *Mmm, mmm, Shard, what have you got yourself into this time? Alone in the woods who-the-hell-knows-where with who-the-hell-knows-what. There're bears in the woods, you know. Cougars, too...*

"Stop it!" he shouted. Then, more quietly, "You're an adult, Buchard. You can do this. You come from good stock. A little out of shape maybe…" He looked down at his belly, hanging like a mushroom cap over his belt. "…but you've got stamina." *And a good store of fat in case you're out here for a while, hmmm?*

"Okay, that's it!" McConnell leapt up from the tree trunk and glanced about frantically—first down the narrow roadbed, then up toward his uncertain destination. He stood frozen to the ground, eyes shut tightly until his pulse stopped pounding in his ears.

Taking a deep breath, he looked back in the direction of the tiny store. Nothing there. Nowhere to sleep. The Leatherby place couldn't be too much farther. They had a spare bed. *And food, too. Wouldn't they have food?*

He pulled the folded note from the pocket of his trousers and opened it. The message was brief and to the point.

Dear Malcolm,

Mister McConnell became lost and his car is disabled. That will be dealt with in the morning. Please feed him well and lodge him for the night. We'll square things later.

E. F.

Feed you well, Shard. Things will seem a lot brighter when your belly's full again. "Damn straight they will," he said to himself, starting back up the road with a new energy in his step.

After another twenty minutes, he rounded a gentle curve in the road and saw the house sitting some fifty yards ahead at the back edge of a sloping meadow. Beyond the house, the terrain rose sharply. Flanking the main structure were two wooden outbuildings that might have housed tools or stores of feed and grain for livestock. McConnell saw no large animals, though, only a few scrawny chickens pecking and scratching in the dusty front yard.

Other movement caught his eye and he glanced to the far side of the main house where a young boy and girl stood staring in his direction. He waved, then watched as the boy scrambled up the steps and into the house. A moment later, a man appeared in the doorway.

"Hello!" McConnell shouted. "Mister Love sent me!"

The man motioned him over and started down the steps. They stopped a few feet apart and exchanged greetings. He was younger than Love, but had the same lean look about him.

"Mister Love sent me," McConnell said again, offering the note in explanation.

The man read the note quickly then offered his hand. "Welcome, Mister McConnell. I'm Malcolm Leatherby and you're just in time for supper." The girl moved to his side and he tilted his head toward her. "This here's my daughter, Hannah, and that's my son, Warren, there on the porch."

The girl was older than McConnell had first thought—fifteen maybe, and blossoming all over with newfound womanhood. A pretty thing with hair the pale yellow of the meadow, she smiled shyly and averted her eyes. McConnell tore his own eyes away from her and nodded at the boy who was perhaps a couple of years younger and blond like his sister.

"Wash up before you eat?" Leatherby asked.

"What? Oh, yes, certainly. I'm a bit grungy from all the walking I've done."

Leatherby pointed to an upright barrel stationed at the corner of the house. "Over there. Stored rainwater. Good for the skin." Leatherby glanced at the girl again. "Go get Mister McConnell a fresh towel, Hannah, and tell your momma we're having a guest for the night."

At the rain barrel, McConnell removed the sweater he'd tied over his shoulders hours ago and turned to see the others disappearing into the house. He thrust his hands into the water and splashed it up into his face. God, it felt good! He glanced back at the house again, quickly stripping off his shirt and splashing more of the cool water over his upper body and under his arms. He finished by ducking his entire head into the barrel, leaving it there until he had to come up for air.

He took a deep breath and wiped the water from his face. When he opened his eyes, Hannah stood six feet away, watching him. He reached for the sweater and held it to his chest. "I didn't know you were there."

Her eyes flickered over his half-clothed body and color rose in her cheeks.

McConnell glanced quickly back toward the deserted front porch then ran one hand through his dripping hair. "How old are you, Hannah?"

"Fourteen." She lifted her chin defiantly for a moment, then lowered it and looked up at him through feathery, corn silk eyelashes. "But I'm mature for my age."

McConnell let his eyes do a little roaming of their own and felt a growing warmth in his loins. "Yes, I can see that."

She thrust a towel in his direction. "Momma says supper's ready."

He took the towel and watched as the girl walked back to the house. *Now that is what you'd call a succulent morsel. Careful, though. Does the term "jailbait" strike a familiar note?*

He sighed and slipped the sweater over his head. It was a favorite—brown with small, black vertical stripes. He thought it had a slimming effect and was glad he'd brought it along.

Mouth-watering cooking smells met him on the front porch and he was about to rap on the door frame when an older version of the daughter appeared in the doorway.

"I'm Olivia, Mister McConnell, Malcolm's wife. C'mon in the house." She opened the door wide and stepped back to let him pass. "My, but you're a robust fellow aren't you? I'll bet you're starving." She took small, quick steps over to the table and pulled out a chair. "Please, sit."

He sat across the table from Hannah and Warren—Malcolm and Olivia at the opposite ends. The surface of the table was covered with bowls of steaming vegetables, a platter of smoked sausage links, and cornbread. Saliva formed at the corners of his mouth and he wiped it away with his fingers.

"You have a garden?" he asked. "I didn't see one."

"Nope," Malcolm answered. "It's too hilly and rocky for more'n a tomato plant or two and a few peppers. We trade with E. F. down at the store. Get most of our vegetables there, swap him some game from time to time."

Olivia nodded at Malcolm and the family joined hands. She smiled and held her other hand out to McConnell. "Join us for the blessing?" He took her hand and glanced at Malcolm, who extended his hand as well.

Heads bowed and Malcolm began. "Lord, bless this food that we are about to receive. Use it to the good of our bodies, so that we may gain strength to serve you better. Amen."

"Amen." Olivia echoed. She gave McConnell's hand a gentle squeeze and unfolded her napkin. "Don't be bashful now. Help yourself."

He did just that, taking a generous helping of each item and two squares of cornbread slathered with butter. He bit into a moist sausage link and juice ran down over his chin. Wiping it away with his napkin, he nodded enthusiastically at Olivia.

"Mmm … great," he said. She smiled at him and he thought she might have blushed a little.

Between mouthfuls, he answered questions about his job as a contributing editor – *nothing wrong with a little embellishment now and then, right, Shard?* – and this job in particular.

"It wasn't actually an assignment. I'm doing this story on my own. As a journalist, you have to do your own investigating, you know. Track down leads, go wherever they take you, find folks who can supply facts that make the story interesting—make it *great*. That's what I was doing…" McConnell tried to think of a positive spin for his current predicament, but failed. "…until I got lost and had the problem with the car."

"All on your own?" Olivia asked. "Couldn't that be dangerous? I mean, what if you came across a moonshine still? Up in these hills, you might get yourself shot."

"Maybe, but I can take care of myself. I'm pretty strong and I've gotten through some tough scrapes before." *Well, sure you have. You handled that thing with the car today, didn't you? As a matter of fact, it's all working out pretty well.* He glanced quickly at Hannah.

She was watching him. He'd caught her at it a couple of times. Not that it meant anything. Probably don't get many visitors way up here. *But you're still a little flattered aren't you. A young thing like that...*

Malcolm pushed back from the table and stood. "I suspect you're mighty tired after your long day, Mister McConnell. If you're ready, I'll show you your room." He stepped into a narrow hallway and McConnell followed. "Here you go," he said, opening the door to a small, tidy bedroom. On a rough-hewn night table beside the bed, a candle glowed softly. "In the morning, we'll get you fixed up right. For now, I think you'll be comfortable enough here." With that, Malcolm nodded and closed the door.

McConnell tested the bed. It was surprisingly soft. *It's a featherbed, Shard. You'll sink to the bottom and never come up.* But when he lay down, he was asleep in seconds, dreaming of pretty blonde fairies with gossamer wings.

He awoke early to a rooster crowing. "Damn," he muttered, "that's worse than an alarm clock." He sat up, stretched, and rubbed his eyes. *Is that biscuits you smell? Don't want to be late for breakfast—that'd be downright rude.* He opened the door and walked down the hallway. Hannah and Warren sat at the table, hands clasped in front of them, looking expectant.

Like they were waiting for you.

Olivia looked up from her wood burning stove and said, "Well, good morning, sleepyhead. We were wonderin' if you were going to be awake in time for breakfast. Malcolm's eaten already, tending to chores. Would you like some eggs and biscuits? Afterward, Hannah and Warren will walk you down to Love's store. They catch the school bus there."

McConnell's stomach growled noisily. "You bet! I'll need some nourishment for my trip."

Olivia took a basket from under the cabinet and handed it to her daughter. "Take Mister McConnell and y'all gather some eggs from the hen house." Smiling sweetly at her overnight guest, she added, "You have to work for your food in this household."

Hannah stood waiting by the door, a mischievous grin playing across lips that looked like ripe cherries.

McConnell said, "No problem."

He followed the girl to the structure at the right of the house. It was close to fifteen feet tall and about twelve feet wide and deep. A low door, hinged on the side, appeared to provide the only access.

"We'll have to go in through there," Hannah said, handing him the basket. "I'll go through first; you can follow." She got down on her hands and knees and ducked under the door.

McConnell watched intently as the young girl crawled through the passageway, the thin cotton dress outlining the contours of her hips. *Oh, sweet Jesus, Shard.* He began to ache with desire.

"You can give me the basket now," she called back through the opening.

He knelt in front of the doorway and peered inside. A covered wooden chute, two to three feet long, opened out into a dim interior. Straw-filled nest rows lined the rear wall—all he could actually see from his position—and a faintly fetid smell filled his nostrils. Inside, Hannah sat hunkered down on her heels, arms around her knees, a sliver of bare thigh gleaming from under her dress.

"Come on in," she said.

McConnell's breath caught in his throat. He tossed the basket through, tucked his head down, and inched forward on all fours. It was a tight fit. *A tight fit... hmmm. What sort of image does that bring to mind, stud?* He had half of his body stuffed into the enclosure, his face six inches from the straw-covered dirt floor, when a pang of claustrophobia hit him. "I'm not sure I can get through."

"Sure you can." Hannah laughed. "Just wiggle."

McConnell dug in with the toes of his shoes and pushed as hard as he could. Took a breath. Pushed again. Half a minute later, his head and shoulders cleared the top of the chute and he could see Hannah again. She was smiling at him.

"See," she said. "I knew you could do it."

He smiled back at her and when she glanced up over his head, he tilted his own face up to follow her gaze.

Oh, Shard...

The eight-pound sledge hammer connected with McConnell's forehead at a velocity of almost ten feet per second. He dropped like a cow in a slaughterhouse.

Malcolm Leatherby stepped down off the chute and, struggling just a little, pulled the body free of the passageway. McConnell's eyes were fixed and dull already and there was an inch-deep indentation midway between them and the line of curly brown hair. Malcolm maneuvered a chain and pulley device out into the center of the room, placing a large washtub underneath. "Go out the side door, Hannah, and fetch Warren to come help me with the lifting. Oh, and may as well tell your momma to fire up the smokehouse as soon as she finishes in the kitchen. This part won't take too long."

The girl was almost through the door when her father called to her. "You did good, honey. You're a real asset to the family."

Down in the hollow later that morning, Earle Franklin Love shook hands with his nephew and watched the junkyard truck disappear down the road with the Dodge Colt in tow. The little car would be stripped and crushed, an unrecognizable lump of scrap metal before noon. He studied the side of the mountain for a moment, saw a trail of smoke from the Leatherby place, then turned and went back inside.

Mavis looked up from her paperback.

Love tapped his pipe into an ash tray and leaned on the counter. "Better make room in the freezer, darlin'. Looks like we'll be stocking winter meat."

Customers

Zdravka Evtimova

Few customers visit my shop. They watch the animals in the cages and seldom buy them. The room is narrow and there is no place for me behind the counter, so I usually sit on my old moth-eaten chair behind the door. Hours I stare at frogs, lizards, snakes and insects. Teachers come and take frogs for their biology lessons; fishermen drop in to buy some kind of bait; that is practically all. Soon, I'll have to close my shop and I'll be sorry about it, for the sleepy, gloomy smell of formalin has always given me peace and an odd feeling of home. I have worked here for five years now.

One day a strange small woman entered my room. Her face looked frightened and grey. She approached me, her arms trembling, unnaturally pale, resembling two dead white fish in the dark. The woman did not look at me, nor did she say anything. Her elbows reeled, searching for support on the wooden counter. It seemed she had not come to buy lizards and snails; perhaps she had simply felt unwell and looked for help at the first open door she happened to notice. I was afraid she would fall and took her by the hand. She remained silent and rubbed her lips with a handkerchief. I was at a loss; it was very quiet and dark in the shop.

"Have you moles here?" she suddenly asked. Then I saw her eyes. They resembled old, torn cobwebs with a little spider in the centre, the pupil.

"Moles?" I muttered. I had to tell her I never had sold moles in the shop and I had never seen one in my life. The woman wanted to hear something else - an affirmation. I knew it by her eyes; by the timid stir of her fingers that reached out to touch me. I felt uneasy staring at her.

"I have no moles," I said. She turned to go, silent and crushed, her head drooping between her shoulders. Her steps were short and uncertain.

"Hey, wait!" I shouted. "Maybe I have some moles." I don't know why I acted like this.

Her body jerked, there was pain in her eyes. I felt bad because I couldn't help her.

"The blood of a mole can cure sick people," she whispered. "You only have to drink three drops of it."

I was scared. I could feel something evil lurking in the dark.

"It eases the pain at least," she went on dreamily, her voice thinning into a sob.

"Are you ill?" I asked. The words whizzed by like a shot in the thick moist air and made her body shake. "I'm sorry."

"My son is ill."

Her transparent eyelids hid the faint, desperate glitter of her glance. Her hands lay numb on the counter, lifeless like firewood. Her narrow shoulders looked narrower in her frayed grey coat.

"A glass of water will make you feel better," I said.

She remained motionless and when her fingers grabbed the glass her eyelids were still closed. She turned to go, small and frail, her back hunching, her steps noiseless and impotent in the dark. I ran after her. I had made up my mind.

"I'll give you blood of a mole!" I shouted.

The woman stopped in her tracks and covered her face with her hands. It was unbearable to look at her. I felt empty. The eyes of the lizards sparkled like pieces of broken glass. I didn't have any mole's blood. I didn't have any moles. I imagined the woman in the room, sobbing. Perhaps she was still holding her face with her hands. Well, I closed the door so that she could not see me, then I cut my left wrist with a knife. The wound bled and slowly oozed into a little glass bottle. After ten drops had covered the bottom, I ran back to the room where the woman was waiting for me.

"Here it is", I said. "Here's the blood of a mole."

She didn't say anything, just stared at my left wrist. The wound still bled slightly, so I thrust my arm under my apron. The woman glanced at me and kept silent. She did not reach for the glass bottle, rather she turned and hurried toward the door. I overtook her and forced the bottle into her hands.

"It's blood of a mole!"

She fingered the transparent bottle. The blood inside sparkled like dying fire. Then she took some money out of her pocket.

"No. No," I said.

Her head hung low. She threw the money on the counter and did not say a word. I wanted to accompany her to the corner. I even poured another glass of water, but she would not wait. The shop was empty again and the eyes of the lizards glittered like wet pieces of broken glass.

Cold, uneventful days slipped by. The autumn leaves whirled hopelessly in the wind, giving the air a brown appearance. The early winter blizzards hurled snowflakes against the windows and sang in my veins. I could not forget that woman. I'd lied to her. No one entered my shop and in the quiet dusk I tried to imagine what her son looked like. The ground was frozen, the streets were deserted and the winter tied its icy knot around houses, souls and rocks.

One morning, the door of my shop opened abruptly. The same small grey woman entered and before I had time to greet her, she rushed and embraced me. Her shoulders were weightless and frail, and tears were streaking her delicately wrinkled cheeks. Her whole body shook and I thought she would collapse, so I caught her trembling arms. Then the woman grabbed my left hand and lifted it up to her eyes. The scar of the wound had vanished but she found the place. Her lips kissed my wrist, her tears made my skin warm. Suddenly it felt cosy and quiet in the shop.

"He walks!" The woman sobbed, hiding a tearful smile behind her palms. "He walks!"

She wanted to give me money; her big black bag was full of different things that she had brought for me. I could feel the woman had braced herself up, her fingers had become tough and stubborn. I accompanied her to the corner but she only stayed there beside the street-lamp, looking at me, small and smiling in the cold.

It was so cosy in my dark shop and the old, imperceptible smell of formalin made me dizzy with happiness. My lizards were so beautiful that I loved them as if they were my children.

In the afternoon of the same day, a strange man entered my room. He was tall, scraggly and frightened.

"Have you... the blood of a mole?" he asked, his eyes piercing through me. I was scared.

"No, I haven't. I have never sold moles here."

"Oh, you have! You have! Three drops... three drops, no more... My wife will die. You have! Please!"

He squeezed my arm.

"Please... three drops! Or she'll die..."

My blood trickled slowly from the wound. The man held a little bottle and the red drops gleamed in it like embers. Then the man left and a little bundle of bank-notes rolled on the counter.

On the following morning a great whispering mob of strangers waited for me in front of my door. Their hands clutched little glass bottles.

"Blood of a mole! Blood of a mole!"

They shouted, shrieked, and pushed each other. Everyone had a sick person at home and a knife in his hand.

Mucca   Karen Beatty

"Moooka!" For the startle effect Richie Visconti raced diagonally across the street to cut in front of the girl. He popped his eyes in her face and extended the "Moo" in a deep, resonate voice to emulate the cow sound. We were not yet teenagers in 1956 but we all knew that "Mucca" meant "cow" in Italian, and that "cow" meant slob or loose woman in English.

On my way to our neighborhood school, dragging 30 feet behind Mucca so that I wouldn't be identified with her in any way, I felt shame rising like heated mercury, tingeing my face red. I saw Mucca grip her books to her chest and drop her head. Euphemistically speaking, she was a *big-boned* girl, yet she seemed to cower inside her ample body. Her dun-colored hair hung as limp and lifeless as the upended mop in the janitor's closet at school. Mucca's blouses were faded and stained; tight balls of lint clung to her garments like dried up chicken pox on skin after the fever has passed. She wore her skirt belted high, and though it was looser and longer than the form fitting just-below-the-knee style of the time, it did not hide her protruding belly, blotchy skin or bulging ankles. In those days girls did not wear pants, and there was no such thing as the polyester over-shirt.

Smirking after delivering his verbal assault on hapless Mucca, Richie dashed back across the street to rejoin his buddies Mikey and Bobby DeCarlo, who were guffawing loudly and pointing at him. The three boys slapped and punched each other to reassure Richie Visconti—and themselves—that they were the better, the cooler, the more popular guys in our elementary school. None of them were very bright, but Richie had good hair and a confident swagger and the DeCarlos, who were fraternal twins, did a lot of clowning around, making up in volume for what they lacked in wit.

Though my empathy was with Mucca, I defensively glanced at the boys and smiled. They ignored me, which was as close to a reprieve as I could get. I was fortunate enough to have two athletic brothers, and, though we were not particularly close, their existence served as a semi-permeable membrane between me and the cruel taunts of the budding young gender assassins. Skinny and shabbily dressed, I knew that I could readily become a target. Mucca was the sacrificial prey who spared me and several other pre-adolescent girls from the cruel epithets of the young bullies. I was only eleven years old, but I knew that Mucca was being abused by those boys. Later I came to understand that the boys assumed such bullying and bravado to obscure their own diminutive statures and dismal prospects. At the time, of course, my perceptions were almost pre-verbal and my behavior was predicated on my own instinct for survival. Sadly, I lacked the imagination, the courage, the wherewithal to affect the dynamics, to make a difference for any of us, especially Mucca.

Of course, Mucca wasn't her real name. I knew very well that the girl's name was Doris Cornell. She, Richie, and the DeCarlo boys lived in the west end of town, where blue collar families like mine, mostly Italian, Polish, or Irish, had settled. Though we never thought about it as such, deprivation was something we all routinely experienced. In the 1950's if you were small-town poor and likely also maltreated, one way to elevate your estate was to create a verbal pecking order to harass those who were clearly worse off than you. Behind each other's backs we kids even referred to our friends from different ethnic groups as "Guinea", "Wap", "Pollack", or "Mick". It required a somewhat more disparate deviance, however, to get you labeled in a way that made you completely socially ostracized. Mucca's family was worse off than most, and she was also guilty of being overweight, ill-kempt, and female. I knew the taunts the boys hurled at her were cruel, but I never publicly acknowledged that; hence, my secret shame: silence is complicity. I intuited this long before I studied the holocaust.

It wasn't just children who were subjected to the scorn and ridicule of our hometown hooligans. There was the rot-toothed "old lady" (likely not more than 35 years old), a single parent raising a shy and mentally deficient son, the boy perpetually, silently, stationed at her side. Their house was dirty—or so we imagined—and stray cats insinuated themselves on their doorstep. I secretly felt sorry for the pair, but joined the other children in dubbing them "The Cat Lady and the Bell Boy." I'm certain that the woman and her son were tormented relentlessly by our giggling and whispering in their presence.

The taunting wasn't entirely sexist, either. Boys in our neighborhood could become the objects of mockery almost as readily as girls. I particularly recall Dumb Danny Domby and his god-forsaken family. His slovenly, toothless mother looked like one of our grannies and his red-faced old man was a chronic drunk who ranted incessantly in slurred obscenities while abjectly beating up on his wife and son. Simultaneously bemused and horrified, we kids gathered beneath their apartment window and listened to the raging and howling within. If Danny managed to escape midst one of these episodes, we chased after him, cheering and applauding. He actually savored the chase—I guess it was some kind of personal acknowledgement.

One Christmas season at school Dumb Danny got in trouble with the teacher and had to stay in the classroom while the rest of us went out for recess on the playground. Suddenly there was a loud gasp from the teacher; we followed her gaze to the roof of the school building. There was Danny Domby poised on the roof, hoisting above his head the Christmas tree our class had spent hours decorating with handmade paper ornaments and the teacher's delicate glass ones. A stand-off quickly developed: Danny threatening to heave the tree; the teacher, joined by other teachers, the janitor and the principal, all cajoling Danny to put down the tree. Some of the little girls on the playground started to cry, about the welfare of the Christmas tree, of course, not Danny Domby. Many children, like me, stood by in stunned silence, while the ruffians shouted for Danny to throw the tree and jump. I could tell Danny was frozen in irresolution. The principal, not much of a negotiator, soon shouted, "That's it for you Domby, we're coming up." With that, Danny stepped forward to the edge of the roof and hurled the tree, in all its ornamented glory, off the roof. The tree tilted slightly sideways, and, as bits of colorful paper and glass orbs whipped away, fell with a thud-bounce-squash on the blacktop of the playground.

"Oooooh-wa!," came the communal cry from the kids below, followed by applause and some whimpers. Danny turned and dashed across the roof, down the back stairwell and out the rear of the school building. The janitor and the gym teacher scampered in pursuit. We didn't see Danny at school again until after the holidays. Whatever punishment was meted out by the principal likely paled in comparison to what he got from his daddy. The incident was talked about and enacted animatedly for years, and Danny Domby accrued a modicum of prestige from the notoriety.

While at the time I lacked the means and mettle to confront social injustices, I was generally sympathetic to the more vulnerable children from our end of town. When no one was looking, I would, from time to time, talk to Doris Cornell. She was grateful, but could never meet my eyes. I also remember a young man oddly named Gaston, whose family had fled Cuba and settled in New Jersey. I was clueless to the politics but knew there was something special about his bearing, something different from the other Spanish kids we called "Spics", who predominantly lived in the next town over. Gaston taught himself brilliant English by watching TV, and his aspirations were beyond most of ours. There were also Jewish kids whom I befriended, mostly at school. They lived on the east end of town and were generally smarter and economically better off than the west end kids. Most of the Jewish kids kept to themselves and did not "come out" as Jews in the Christian-dominated working class milieu of our town. While they enjoyed the cache (and economic advantages) of living on the east side of town, the Jewish kids were still outsiders.

Within the prevailing social strata, I must have been a rather difficult person to peg. At school I hung out with the more academically-oriented youngsters from the east end, but after school and on weekends I was solidly west end. That made me not so much a social isolate as a loner. I navigated the great barrier reef of the social domain like a hyper-alert minnow—now a flash of silver, now camouflaged, hovering in the nooks and crannies, snatching for bits and scraps and eluding the bottom feeders.

Eventually Danny Domby's family moved away from the west end, likely to a different emerging urban region of the Garden State. By eighth grade Richie Visconti had gotten "sent up the river" (our slang for remanded to reform school), where he attained rapid promotion from within, eventually ending up at Rahway State Prison. One of the DeCarlo brothers was killed in the early days of the Vietnam War, and the other, the last I heard, had opened up a pizza joint at the Jersey shore.

I still wonder what happened to Doris Cornell. Did she, like I, move away from "our town" and reinvent herself? The odds were very much against her. We knew that her father was an alcoholic who beat her, but it wasn't until she was discernibly pregnant that people realized she was enduring more than beatings at the hands of the man. Even though the local boys claimed that Mucca "put out", that was highly unlikely. No, her drunken father had, early on, claimed her for himself.

How Doris Cornell must have suffered! To my knowledge, no social service agencies or child advocates ever stepped in on her behalf. The great poet Langston Hughes was soon to pose the question, "What happens to a dream deferred?" My question remains, "What happens to a living nightmare daily sustained?"

Growing up I thought my secret shame would be my home life, where my mother was childlike, at times delusional, but with a core of obstinate resiliency. In the 1950's my father treated her like most working class men treated pesky women and so-called incorrigible children: he screamed at her and slapped or punched her when she got on his last nerve. Eventually I came to terms with both my parents—with a little help from my friends and a few professionals, of course. So my secret shame is not my crazy parents. What is lodged in the back lot of my mind, like one of those non-biodegradable synthetics among decaying debris, is an image of me standing immobilized at a safe distance from Doris Cornell—she a pathetic, wounded animal, arrows protruding. I hope by some miracle Doris prevailed. I hope she found it in her heart to forgive some of us. "Moooka!" The derisive echo persists.

A Palm Reading   K. Bond

October 2008

      Haley tilted the rearview mirror down to apply coral lipstick. The flat tube circled her lips twice to ensure color in every crevice. With her finger, she brushed a minor slip-up from her whitened teeth.

      Haley's sister, Madge, rolled her eyes and swept the glazed donut crumbs from her black sweatpants onto the car mat. "Lipstick is no use when you are over the age of fifty."

      "It's no use when you are over age fifty and dress like that!" Haley snapped the lipstick closed and fluffed her big hair. "Besides, lipstick makes me feel good about myself."

      Madge opened the car door and climbed out. She leaned down and looked at Haley, who was still fussing with her appearance. "If you knew the palm reader was a female, would you still put on lipstick? No, you wouldn't. Don't lie and say you would."

      Finally, Haley emerged from the Altima. She looked over the car's roof at her sister. "My hairdresser told me *her* name is Arabella. Everyone swears she is Indiana's best palm reader. She foretold my hairdresser would come into money. That weekend, she drove to the casino and won five hundred dollars!"

      "Coinc…" Madge began.

      Haley talked over the skeptical comment she anticipated from her sister. "It is just for fun! You could use some more fun in your life. All you do is sit on the couch and watch TV since Bill died."

      Madge circled round the car and stood at Haley's side. "If Arabella starts talking like Bill, I'm gonna slap her. Just warning ya."

      The two walked up the creaky stairs to the small wooden porch--painted purple to match the house. Both tried to peek through the window's gauzy curtains as they approached the door.

Tink-tank-tink-tink.

Haley jumped--startled by the loud sound. She looked over at Madge, who busily attempted to shush a wind chime with rock-like crystals hanging from it. The door creaked open. A woman introduced herself as Arabella and welcomed them inside.

Madge found it difficult to guess the woman's age. Her youth seemed evident from the black hair she wore long and straight, hanging like cords down the sides of her face. The taut olive skin also lent to a twenty-something age estimate, but her eyes undermined those clues. They glowed red like those of a white rabbit.

"Are you wearing colored contacts?" Madge blurt out.

Haley, who never wished to be less tactful than Jackie Onassis, called out, "Madge!"

"It is okay. I don't mind when people ask about my eyes. Sometimes I wish they would ask about something else, like my cute shoes." Arabella proudly pointed down to her gold ballet flats. "But I don't mind when they ask about my eyes. Red eyes are a rare genetic variation. I just got lucky... or unlucky. It depends on how you look at it. I consider myself unlucky because my eyesight is very poor as a consquence. In fact, I'm going to have to ask you to put your hand under here while I read your palm." She pointed to an oversized magnifying glass.

Madge quickly backed away and thrust Haley forward. "Oh no, I am just here 'for fun.' My sister is the one who would like her palm read."

Arabella studied Haley's face a moment. Then, she turned to Madge and said, "No, it is you. You are the one who needs to know your destiny. Sit down. I will read your palm for free. Today only, that is."

Madge sat in the chair and extended her palm for Arabella to analyze. The palm reader adjusted the brass arms of the desk-mounted magnifying glass contraption. While she was tracing the line with her finger and hmmming, Madge shot her sister a dirty look.

"It's not good. You will die this time next year." Arabella folded Madge's hand back up and pushed it away like an unwanted meal.

Haley looked apologetically at her awestruck sister. Then, she glared at the palm reader. "How could you say such a thing?"

"Please leave. You smell like death." Arabella snatched up a nearby fireplace bellow and repeatedly flapped it open and closed in Madge's direction, blowing stale air gusts and dust particles in her eyes.

Haley followed Madge out the door, down the steps, and into the Altima. They both quickly snapped their seatbelts into place. Haley put the car in reverse and peeled out of the gravel driveway onto a paved road.

The road offered very little to look at besides telephone poles. After some period of silence, Haley said, "I am sorry I dragged you here."

Madge did not feel the urgency to offer a quick answer. She stared out the car window and thought about the things she had never told Haley, like her doctor's recommendation to receive bypass surgery and her rejection of his recommendation. She thought about his pleas to change her lifestyle, which currently consisted of eating fruit only when in a double crust pie and eating vegetables only when in a breadcrumb covered casserole.

Even though Madge longed to meet Bill in heaven, she hated to leave her sister all alone. Madge finally replied, "What if the palm reader was right? I think I'll make some changes. You know, take better care of myself."

Haley said nothing because she was pleased Madge showed interest in making a positive change, but the expressive and surprised look she gave Madge went unnoticed because Madge fixated on a lone tree's yolky-yellow autumn leaves.

October 2009

Haley charged up the familiar purple stairs to Arabella's house. She pounded on the door until it cracked open slightly to reveal Arabella's red eyes.

"I am not taking appointments today. Call tomorrow." Arabella began to shut the door.

Haley stuck her moccasin slipper in the door to prevent it from closing. "Do you remember me? You read my sister's palm last October. You said she would die in a year."

Arabella opened the door. She squatted down and leaned uncomfortably close to Haley's black sweatpants. She remained uncomfortably close as she slowly rose up to her face. Arabella touched Haley's bare lips and pictured her face as it looked before--with coral colored lips. "Yes, I remember you now. How is your sister?"

"Dead. That's how she is." Haley walked across the threshold of the door and instantly smelled something unsavory cooking. She tried not to let her imagination run too wild about what Arabella might be cooking.

Arabella rubbed her arm, but Haley brushed it off and grabbed Arabella's shoulders. She stared into her glowing red eyes.

"She died—like you said. The thing is, she really tried to change her future. She ate healthy and exercised all year long. Is the future really set in stone? Can it never be changed?"

Arabella pushed Haley's arms down. "She would have died within the month if she hadn't changed!"

A teapot whistled.

Arabella said, "Excuse me." She slipped between hanging bead strands into the kitchen.

Haley did not wait to bid farewell to Arabella. She promptly left. She followed no one out the door, down the steps, and into the Altima. She backed out of the gravel driveway onto a paved road with little more to look at than telephone poles. As she drove, she thought about meeting Madge again in heaven.

After awhile, she fixated on a lone tree's bare, fingerlike branches--tilting her rearview mirror to keep it in her gaze after she passed it by.

In God's Country   Joseph Grant

There are many ways in which to kill. And in war this deficiency in man has been perfected to a horribly efficient degree. Besides the appalling experience from which one never truly recovers, one of the most difficult lessons of any war is the peace that follows. Not that peace is by any means difficult to endure, it is the fragility of it which must be maintained in order to avoid the next conflict that proves the most fleeting. This is also true in the serenity that comes in the form of peace of mind and to this end, Jack Spangler had made it home from the war, but not without leaving pieces of himself back out there, behind the lines.

This is not to say that Lance Corporal Spangler had gotten through the war physically unscathed, for he had not. He had been wounded twice, once seriously and recovered each time only to be sent back to the action. He was classified as "collateral damage" and reverted back with the rest of them. In the old days, getting wounded in such a manner was a soldier's golden ticket home, but no one was going to the wars these days and the military needed as many men and women as could be mustered. With medical technology being what it is at present, Spangler was opened, reassembled, made new with titanium rods and screws and patched up with the military's new idea that no IED or roadside bomb would ever again take the modern soldier completely out of the field.

The war was behind him now, he thought as he wandered the heavily fogged early morning streets of his hometown of Deer Creek, California, a small wedge of suburbia in an otherwise still rural Silicon Valley. He had gotten off the train at the station a mile back, carrying his suitcase and duffle bag, having been dropped off at Union Station in Downtown Los Angeles by a group of naval buddies who had also discharged out of San Pedro.

He was still drunk from an afternoon of revelry and hard partying at the first place he saw across from the depot, Olvera Street. The pedestrian area was a Mecca of little Mexico and he limped into the first bar he found, La Golondrina. It was deep and dark cavernous restaurant with a chiminera that held a fire almost as warm as the colorful frescos upon the wall. It was a lovely place, quite a find off of the touristy street, he thought and it seemed everyone there wanted to buy him a drink and every girl wanted to talk to him but did not want to sleep with him as he had hoped. If any of those beautiful Latinas had taken him to their place and welcomed him back to the United States the way he pictured, it would have been the ultimate soldier's welcome home, he smirked, but those girls were *far too Christian*, he cursed and he was getting far too drunk to properly salute, if they had.

They were willing enough to let him buy them drinks and kiss him and run their hands through his buzz cut at the bar or run their hands up his dress blues, but that was as far as it went as his money dwindled, he groused. Maybe it was the celebrity of it, them being seen with a soldier just back from the war, the same way women behaved around police or firemen. He was just another man in uniform, it didn't really matter who the man was, as long as there was a uniform. He could have been a serial killer for all they knew and in a sense he was, but he was sanctioned by and given absolution by the government to do so, so no one thought twice about it and called him a hero. That was the crazy part about it. No one even blinked when he admitted he liked killing the enemy.

It had taken him nearly the entire night to catch a train close enough in which he could transfer at two stations to get back home, but he was finally in the place he had dreamt about many nights in the foxhole. It was surreal being back, walking the quiet, sleepy streets once more and he wondered why in hell he had rushed back. As he walked further into town and passed by the closed businesses with the boarded up windows, he wondered what he had been thinking wanting to come back so soon to a place he had always planned on escaping first chance he got.

9/11 and the military had provided that chance. He was still in school when that whole catastrophe went down and his whole fragile mindset was shaped by seeing it happen on TV and its aftermath. His family, fracturing at the time, although he didn't know it, rode the wave of fervent patriotism in shock and awe with the rest of the country. As soon as he was able, he kept a promise to himself and enlisted. Almost immediately after basic, he was shipped out and pulled an endless series of tours in places he had never heard of before. He would fight in historic battles that would soon become familiar to those that followed the war in Iraq and Afghanistan. Battles such as Ramallah, Operation Base Lane in the Zabul province, Tora Bora or Operation Mountain Fire in Barge Matal; working with the CIA paramilitary in Operation Anaconda and to train the newbie ISAF's that came onboard. Spangler remembered becoming annoyed in one of the bars when one of the embedded reporters, a well-known cable news correspondent, recounted the battle of Ramallah as if he'd personally been there when nearly everyone knew he stayed inside the safe Green Zone and even went to so far as to correct Spangler, just because he had read about it in *Time* or *Newsweek*!

    Spangler shook his head at the memory as he hobbled the long, empty columns of sidewalk towards his old school which was due to open in a few hours, he smiled. He had spent many useless hours there in captive audience with many a failed orator and useless human being who sought to impart their curriculum by subjugation and cruelty resulting from their own shortcomings rather than by any intellectual means. Spangler recalled that the parking lot taught him more about life and what to expect, whether it was from the girls he scored with in his car between classes or the pot that was smoked or the fights he won and lost. It was terrible to think of school as just a building, but if it was filled with instructors who had already given up on themselves, how could they ever teach with enough veracity and get through to their impressionable students, he wondered?

    He trudged along in the chill, as the seasons were changing and it was finally then that he spotted the house he grew up in and he contemplated how much had changed since he had last been home. While he was fighting for his country, his father had died of lymphoma, no doubt a souvenir of his days spent working with chemicals at the textile plant and his mother had been showing early signs of dementia. His brother had turned gay and his sister had married a so-called "bad boy" and as a result, had endured a rocky relationship that translated into an equally abusive marriage where she somehow managed to have a baby girl in the midst of this loser's various prison stays. He left

51

her for a lengthier sentence other than marriage and subsequently divorced her, but only after getting her hooked on meth. His excuse being that he had found God while in the correctional facility and as a result, couldn't have a wife who was addicted to drugs. *One man's family*, mused Spangler as he walked along. He recalled one of his brother's letters saying his sister was now strung-out and living with some equally amped-up tattooed biker in Arizona and if he had read in between the lines correctly, she was now hooking to support both their habits. He sighed as he reached the front door. More had changed than just the seasons around here, he mused.

His mother answered the door or rather, a washed-out contrast of what once was. She seemed to have aged considerably since his last leave. She closed over her bathrobe, opened the door and gave him a quizzical look for half a second and then the old recognition returned to her face and she smiled and unlocked the door. Jack followed her down the hallway, his boots plodding noisily behind the patter of his mother's silky slippers. As he reached the kitchen, pulled out a chair with a squeak and sat down, his mother began to prepare coffee.

"It's so good to have you home again, Jacky, in one piece." She said as he noticed how worn out she appeared in the stark fluorescent kitchen light.

"...'s good to be home." He said quietly.

"I thought you were getting out *next* month." She wondered aloud.

"No, it was yesterday, Ma. " He sighed. "I wrote you all about it in the last letter."

"Oh, you're right, *you're right*." She smiled. "It's good to have you home, Jacky." She repeated.

Jack ignored her. "Hey, Ma...you got any of that French toast I like in the freezer?"

"Let me check." She said and walked over to a freezer door that was covered with magnets. There was a child's drawing of blue flowers in a field and an orange sun and what looked like a giant in blood red held up by a 9/11 magnet that read: "Never Forget". Jack smiled at the drawing.

"You know, I could always make you homemade French toast." She said as she looked through the freezer and started to unpack frozen corn and peas onto the counter.

"Nah, I don't want you to go to any trouble, Ma."

"It wouldn't be any trouble, Jacky." She smiled.

"If you have the store-bought, I'll take that. I love that stuff."

"Oh, but Nick."

"Jacky, Ma."

"Oh, yes, I'm sorry." She said. "It's uh, it's probably old." She said as she pulled out the familiar red box and turned it over to look for the expiration date.

"That's all right, Ma. I've been eating C-rations for the last two years. I like the way this stuff tastes, old or not. I like the way you make it." He smiled. "Reminds me of being a kid."

"This is probably here from the last time you were on leave."

"It doesn't matter."

"Please, let me make you home made. It'll take me just a minute." She said and started to unpack the refrigerator onto the counter.

"Ma, would you forget about the home made French toast and just use the store bought?" He snapped.

"Sure, Jacky, sure. You don't have to raise your voice."

"I'm sorry, Ma." He said somewhat ashamed. "But you're making a big deal about me being home and all and I just wanna relax, ya know?" He explained as his mother read the directions of the store bought. "Just put them in the toaster, Ma."

She looked up and at him and put the box on the counter. She began to wring her hands. "How're you doing, Jacky?" She asked. "They feeding you okay?" She said and pulled out three slices and put them in the toaster and pressed the button down. "You look a little skinny."

"Yeah, I'm fine, Ma." He nodded. "How are you? You still having that lady coming by looking after you?"

"I'm okay. I have my good days and my bad. The doctor's got me on this new prescription. I'm okay, like anyone. You mean, Mrs. Mitchell?" She said as her demeanor changed. "I think I'm going to have to get someone else."

"Why?" He said exasperated. "I thought you liked this one?"

"I think she's stealing from me, Jacky. I can't seem to find anything anymore. Little things. I'm finding them in the strangest places. Places I know I didn't put them. Last week, I found fifteen dollars stuffed in the icebox. I think she's stealing and then when she hears me coming, she shoves things where they don't belong. The other day I found my bedroom remote in the sock drawer. Things like that."

"What would she want with your remote?" He wondered.

"I don't know, Nick, uh, Jacky."

"All right, if it will make you feel any better, I'll check up on it." He said as the toaster dinged and spit out three slices of toast. Jack jumped up and prepared it the way he liked it, margarine and lots of sugar and cinnamon, but no syrup and then noticed the corn and peas still on the counter thawing. With the clock ticking loudly in the afterthought of silence, he quietly walked over and placed them back into the freezer as his mother stared ahead and tapped her fingers upon the placemat in front of her.

"Is this Caitlin's?" He asked as the artwork taped on the fridge wavered with the closing of the freezer door.

"Who?"

"Caitlin?" He said. "Your granddaughter?"

"Oh, yes." She turned and nodded. "I know who she is, smartass."

"Uh-huh."

"Yes, that's my little granddaughter. Quite the artist. Just like her grandmother." She sang.

"Uh-huh." Jack said and slunk down again in his seat.

"So, have you thought about what you're going to do now that you're out of the service?"

"Nope."

"That's okay, you still have time to think about things. Maybe I can get you to fix a few things around here."

"Maybe." He said and started to eat.

"I can call up your Dad's old boss, Mr. Murphy. Maybe he can take you on."

"Ma, the textile place closed down years ago. Besides, old man Murphy died years ago. He died before Dad did."

"Oh, you're right. What the hell is wrong with me? Honestly, I swear. What was I thinking, Jacky?" She said and shook her head. "Honestly, I don't know where my mind has been lately. I guess I've been worrying about you." She smiled and rubbed his hand. Jack genuinely returned the smile. For a brief while, it was if she had returned again.

"Have you heard from your brother?"

"Bryce?" Jack asked. "Yeah, he's written me here and there. Talked to him just before I shipped out to come back. He's doing all right."

"I wish he would settle down. He's still living the gay bachelor life, as we used to call it before gay meant something else. Him and his roommate, they should both grow up, settle down with nice girls, if you ask me." She said pointedly.

"I'll see if I can talk to him." Jack lied. *She was closer to the truth than she knew*, he thought.

"You hear from Elaine?"

"Nope."

"She's another one. I don't understand that girl."

"She sent you that drawing?" Jack said absentmindedly.

"Yeah, last year. The only time I hear from her is around her birthday or when her boyfriend beats the hell out of her."

"Ma, she calls you on her birthday for money for drugs." Jack said, no longer wanting to keep the big family secret.

"She told me she was clean this time."

"That's what she always says." Jack griped. "Do yourself a favor, hang up on her the next time she calls, okay?"

"Well, when I start hollering at her, she threatens me that she'll never let me near Caitlin again. Breaks my heart, so I have to try and remember to be nice to her."

"I thought Caitlin was going to be in foster care or something?"

"Well, turns out the family changed their mind once they found out she was from druggie parents. Then, Elaine wanted me to take her but you know I can't, so she pleaded and cried her eyes out to the judge and frankly, I don't know who the bigger jerk is, her or that judge but the stupid judge awarded her custody." She rolled her eyes. "She's my *only* grandchild. It's not like I can depend on you or Bryce before I die." She smacked at Jack's arm, making him drop his fork. "Come on, give Lisa a call."

"Ma, come on." He snarled, remembering all of the drama Lisa had put him through. She was beautiful, with what most women would call a cute figure but that was not what most guys called it, he recalled with a knowing smile. The smile faded as he remembered what a psychotic she was and how as an engagement gift, he bought her a ring and the 300 CCS of augmentation she had always wanted. He recalled how afterwards, she thought she was a centerfold-in-the-making and as a result, never let Jack forget it. She cheated on him while he was in basic and he broke off the engagement and dumped her and remembered how stupid he was to agree to get back together with her. They didn't make attention whores any more desperate than this one and the less attention he could give her, the better.

"Why don't you call her?"

"Leave it alone, Ma." He said as scarfed down and he finished the last of his breakfast.

"Just call her, you'll see."

"I gotta get some air." He said and stood abruptly.

"But the coffee's not even ready." His mother said absently. "Don't leave. You just got here."

"Later, I'll have it later. I gotta get outta here." He snapped and bolted tiredly out of the door. It was against his better judgment, but he needed to remove himself from the situation. He thought about what happened next as he sat with his psychiatrist a month later.

"I went to the bar and had a few more drinks until I could forget about everything for awhile."

"What did you need to forget about?" The man interjected.

"The war, people getting blown up right in front of me, body parts."

"And this bothered you, why?"

"What? What do you mean why? Are you even listening to me?"

"Do you think people don't listen to you, Jack? Do you feel inferior and this is compensated by your need to lash out at those around you, so you can get noticed?"

"What?" Jack snapped. "I think *you're* the one who's crazy."

"Interesting."

"What?"

"Nothing."

"You think *I'm* paranoid now, huh?"

"If *you* say so." The man smiled at his own in-joke.

"So, I was at this bar and this girl walked in."

"And this excited you?"

"Well, sure, yeah, doc. Whatever. So, we started getting talking and comfortable and all and I wanted to get to know her better, ya know, but she wanted to dance and I couldn't on account of my leg."

"Go on."

"She started to mock me about my leg, saying I was probably lying about the war just to go to bed with her and that I probably couldn't dance anyway and this was an excuse. She was a real weird sort of girl. Had a twisted sense of humor." Jack shook his head. "I wanted to go home with her, but she didn't seem too interested or I was getting too drunk again."

"So, you don't think you could have performed?"

"Huh? I don't know. I guess so. I was getting *pretty* drunk."

"Why do you feel the need to drink until intoxication? Can't you drink socially?"

"I don't see the point, if you ask me. I like the way it makes me feel. Like I said, I'm trying to forget about things."

"Why? You knew you were going to be called into combat if you went in the military. It's not much of stretch, Jack." He nodded. "It must have occurred to you at some point-"

"Yes, *thank you* for stating the obvious."

"Do you always feel the need to deal with situations that bother you or upset you with sarcasm?"

"*Maybe.*" He said caustically. "Well, it seemed appropriate."

"So, getting back to this girl you met at the bar...what happened with her?"

"Well, we were talking and I turned on the charm and then the talking led to kissing and then we left in her car. We went back to her place and I remember her making fun of my wounds. Can you believe that?"

"People don't owe you anything because you were wounded."

"But I fought for this country!"

"I'm not saying that. I'm saying don't expect people to give you a break. It's not in their nature. So what happened next?"

"Then I woke up. There was blood but she was nowhere to be found."

"How much blood? A lot? A little?"

"Like a nosebleed or something, but she was gone. I don't know what happened. I'm not sure if she had a nosebleed or maybe it was her time of the month or maybe she was a virgin or something."

"We both can say with an air of certainty she most likely wasn't a virgin."

"I guess." Jack said confusedly. "I think she just split and went to work."

"What makes you say that?"

"Her car was gone."

"Do you think maybe you physically attacked her and then took her car and dumped her and the car somewhere?"

"Stick to what you do best, doc and it isn't police work. Like I said, she was gone."

"And this made you mad?"

"No, it made me feel completely alone. To answer your assumption, I didn't hurt her. At least not that I can remember."

"It's interesting that you forgot. Just like with your mother and her dementia."

"Oh, please. I don't have 'mother' issues."

"*Father issues?*"

"I don't think so."

"Well, I think that being in the war would bring that sense of abandonment to the forefront by your own admission of a distant father to some sort of closure, at least. What do *you* think?"

"Do I think that he'd be proud of me? Yes. Did I join up to heal the wounds between us and close the gap? Sure." Jack acknowledged. "He was in the war. But he never wanted to talk about any of it."

"My father was in the war, too. I thought about joining up to be honest, you know, to make the old man proud, but I went to college instead, got my degree." He pointed to the wall. "You and my old man would've gotten along famously. He *always* talked about his war effort."

"We're here to talk about me, *remember*?" Jack chided him.

The psychiatrist cleared his throat. "War is such a noble endeavor, brings out bravery in man, the cowardice in lesser men. Do you know who said that?"

"No and I don't care. What would *you* know?" Jack exploded. "Sounds to me like you've never seen war except on TV or in the movies. Same with your old man. Anyone who has ever been in real combat doesn't want to talk about it. Sounds like your old man was making up stories, if you ask me. Making himself bigger than he was."

"My father was a great man, I'll have you know."

"Sounds like you're the one with 'Daddy' issues." Jack snickered.

"Mr. Spangler, that will be all for today." He said and cleared his throat. "Until next time?"

"Sure, whatever." Jack stood and walked out, slamming the door behind him as the flimsy wall shook. He was pissed. He didn't even care if the hot MILF secretary he had always wanted to bang thought he was a psycho. The guy she worked for had no business glorifying wholesale slaughter like it was some heroic adventure.

As he walked out of the professional building, past the dry-cleaners, the movie rental store and the pharmacy, he noticed for the first time all of the flags flying and the yellow ribbons attached seemingly to every tree, their imitation silk shamelessly tattered and threadbare and forgotten as the country's patriotism. Everywhere, banners waved with red, white and blue, but even though the expression that people once used was "These Colors Don't Run", the ink that the *Made in China* banners bore had faded with age and exposure to the elements.

He spotted his own banner hanging off of a light pole and climbed up and grabbed at it until he ripped it down. As far as he and the United States Government were concerned, his tour of duty was officially over and this was tantamount to false advertising. A passing police cruiser slowed down but kept going as Jack glared at the young recruit.

He wandered the town he had grown up in and felt alienated from it all. He had gone and seen the world and yet the world that shaped him to be that soldier stayed monotonously the same. Nothing had changed, except for him. The old men still congregated on the benches and watched the world go by and did nothing but age. The girls at the high schools made him think of the dripping, teenaged whores he and his regiment sought comfort with in Afghanistan and it made him turn his head in shame. Surrounded by people he knew all of his life, he never felt so alone in his entire existence.

The buildings, the schools, the shops, the houses, the narrow lawns and minds all stayed the same as if everything had regressed into some sort of Perfect Town, USA and all of them were blissfully unaware of the carnage just outside their border.

Innocuously, people were outside in oversized Havana hats and gardening gloves, watering their lawns or working on their cars wherever he went as butterflies were fluttering and birds chirping in the bright afternoon sunshine while a whole generation was dying overseas. It was if people were blithely oblivious by fault or comfortable design to what was truly going on in the world. Whereas this idyllic scene would have reassured the returning solider, it infuriated Spangler. The peace of mind he sought was nowhere to be found in the small town he dreamt about returning to while on the front lines. Even though he was barely old enough to drink, the worm was already turning inside his fevered mind. Sometimes, he wished he could shoot it all away.

He was unable to find steady work on account of his injuries and it depressed him. No one wanted to hire a veteran who would be out for months at a time because of corrective surgeries and the physical therapy that would follow thereafter. He hated the way people stared at his limp. Only a monthly government check kept his restless head above desperate waters.

He could always go back to the war. That was the thing with man. Man would *always* provide another war to go to. For the time being, ex-Lance Corporal Jack Spangler would remain a casualty of peace; a peace he helped foment. Peace was lousy and monotonous but that was the prize of war, controlled chaos. It was the peace that would prove to be the hardest battle he would ever face. The pills the psychiatrist gave him staved off the rage that boiled inside. He just hoped the war within him would not erupt in the meantime.

Blessed Garden

Esther Poyer

Marsha's feet tread lightly along the pavement like a snare drum beat with a heel thud accompaniment, her right foot swollen from an insect bite. Last evening, after a full day on the busy supermarket shop floor, she had been sitting out in her garden. Still in her leather bomber jacket and scarf from her journey home, she reflected over her Good News Bible, which was rested on her lap and opened to the book of Psalms. She nestled into her fold-a-away camping chair, the cool bluish air nipping around her neck and cheeks.

The newly laid lawn was doing well. She liked its ruffled and slightly unkempt look, with the pink and purple wildlife flowers springing out of the borders, but it wasn't yet the enchanted nirvana she had had in mind. About a month before, she planted a tiny pair of ivy shoots, which were of course still in their infancy. As with her two youngsters, the miniature black green foliage would require nurturing hands to train them. For the ivy, towards disguising the expanse of standard issue dusty apricot colored bricks. For her two teenage charges, guidance through faith, in contemplation of their escape up and over the wall, from the potential ravages, the possible abyss of inner city strife.

Autumn was beginning its customary transformation. A handful of leaves shed from next door's oak tree lay dotted over the lawn, like fallen stars of yellow and orange ochre. In her own vegetable patch, there remained one row of lettuce, the rumpled green of butter head at the front, receding to an auburn flamed mix of oak leaf. They sat proudly, between a tepee of bare bamboo where a sprinkling of pea pods had been plucked and eaten raw over the July to August months, and a wash of spinach that still ran wild, hogging the bed. The strawberry plants had produced the welcome surprise of a ripe red berry every now and then. Marsha had harvested it with excited relish, cutting it into equal thirds for the three of them. Through a veil of mild teenage nihilism, Rodney and Patrice partook in their mother's good life intentions.

They guessed she was also making a point, given that such seemingly random gestures were typical of her.

The itch and irritation in Marsha's swollen foot was like ground pepper seed beneath the dark cinnamon skin of her instep. It mounded, uncomfortable and pushing against the tightening edges of her tartan plimsolls, her feet were slightly hooded by the dark blue of her loose denim jeans. The paving stones were cracked in places, uneven and jutting upwards at the kerb with thick spaced out gaps. The black burnished iron of a stopcock cover formed a dip in the grey granite ground. She skipped over it, wondering when they might come along and inconvenience the residents and road users of Morpeth Way with a *New Pavements Project*. She was sure it would be gladly tolerated if it meant there would be a decent walkway. Perhaps one where people didn't feel so compelled to discard fried chicken boxes, fish and chip papers, and the pint glasses that they had stumbled out of the pub at the end of the road with, dumping them half-filled or empty.

The flat was just a few hundred yards away as she passed beneath a canopy of young silver birch trees. The pavement was heavily soiled with ingested berry bird droppings, dark purple splashes, and grey around the edges. As she crossed the road and passed the St Matthews Methodist Church, she thought about how rain would inevitably pour, and wash away the unsightly bird foul. The perfectly balanced nature of things would take care of it. The change of season, the weather, the sunshine, early morning dew, twilight lit evenings, starry darkness, all the elements that make up the atmosphere flitted through her mind. Despite the sting in her step, she felt a warmth in her chest as a tremor ran down through her shoulders. Suddenly it all made sense. The grace between bitter and sweet, beauty and beast, cosmic and concrete. The matter of taking cues from the universe. When the body is unwashed, weary and in need of replenishment it is bathed. And when the sins of the father prey upon the children, they are baptized.

Up at the plate   Thomas Healy

Humming along with Patsy Cline on the radio, his voice too wretched even for him to listen to, Mayo cruised down the highway in his air-conditioned Jeep Cherokee. Scarcely anyone else was out on the road. It was just too hot, likely to reach a hundred by late afternoon according to the last forecast he heard on the radio. About the only people he noticed the past couple of miles were strawberry pickers, all hunched over in the bright red fields with their cartons and baskets beside them. He smiled, remembering all the summers he had picked berries with his grandparents, wearing one of Pa's stained straw hats that was two sizes too big for his grapefruit-sized head.

"You might look like a scarecrow," Pa laughed the first time he gave him a hat to wear. "But you don't want to get heat stroke, do you?"

"No, sir."

"Take it from me, boyo, it's always better to feel good than look good."

"I guess."

"No guessing about it, boyo. That's a flat out fact."

A little farther on, winding through a tight curve, he approached a road sign that made him cringe. "Seven Oaks," it said. "Next Exit." Urgently he clamped his eyes shut until he was sure he had passed the faded sign. He wished he had not seen it but he knew he would, sooner or later, because where he was headed was in the same direction as Seven Oaks.

As a roving hitting instructor for the Detroit Tigers, he went where he was assigned, and this weekend he was told to report to their affiliate in Winchester---the Winchester Tigers. This was the first season they had been associated with the Class A club. Desperately he tried to wriggle out of the assignment but Mr. Hedgecock, the Director of Player Development, was adamant that he go because the ball club had, by fifteen points, the worst team batting average in the league.

"I'm not a miracle worker," he told Hedgecock.

"No, Mayo, you're not, and I'm not expecting you to be one. But you've got a sharp enough eye to bring up their average three or four points and that'll do for now."

He didn't disagree, convinced he could improve just about any batter's average a few points, but still he didn't want to go to Winchester. It was only twenty-six miles from Seven Oaks, which was definitely the last place he wanted to see again.

*

Mayo, a fungo bat poised on his right shoulder, stood a few feet behind the chipped plate and watched a young outfielder swing at balls thrown by the rickety pitching machine. The kid had what an old manager of his called "a spidery swing" because it was all over the place. He watched him take less than a dozen swings but that was enough for him to conclude the kid would not advance beyond Class A ball. Still, he had to offer some advice, which he suspected the kid would take as encouragement, because that was his job.

"You're very busy in the box," he told him as a ball boy reloaded the pitching machine. "So if I were you I'd be a little quieter. More relaxed, if you will."

The kid, knocking some dirt from his cleats, appeared confused by his comment.

"Don't be so fidgety when you're in the batter's box. Be like you are in church. Be still. Stillness is what'll give you results."

"I am still."

"No, son, you're not. You're moving around as if you've got an itch you can't scratch. Just stand still and be ready to swing and you'll get more wood on the ball."

"If you say so," he sighed, urgently tapping the plate with the head of his bat.

*

Mayo had earned a living in baseball almost half his life. He signed with the Tigers straight out of high school. A catcher in school, he was soon converted to a first baseman, and there he played for four and a half seasons until he tore a tendon sliding into home and subsequently was released. He got as far as

Double A ball. His career in baseball seemingly was through before he was twenty-three but one of his managers appreciated his knack for analyzing the strengths and weaknesses of batters and recommended him for a scouting position. Eager to stay in the game, he took it and slowly advanced through the organization, scouting mainly but also for the past two years working as a hitting instructor. He never hit very well himself, batting scarcely above his weight with six home runs in a total of 182 games, but for some reason he was adept at identifying the flaws in other swings and suggesting corrections.

Other than hitting a ball what he liked most about baseball was talking about hitting with young prospects. So he was always excited when he was sent out to one of the farm clubs to offer some instruction, but not this time. Not here in Winchester. He'd rather be anywhere but here, even in Alaska if the team had an affiliation there.

*

Mayo stood with Clete Holcomb, the manager of the Winchester club, behind the batting cage and watched a lanky kid line balls deep into the corner of left field. As usual, a cigarette hung from his lower lip, dribbling ashes across the front of his atrocious Hawaiian shirt.

"So what do you think of Earl?" Clete asked after the young slugger crushed a ball off the left field wall.

"Oh, he's got the tools all right," Mayo answered. "His wrists are lightning fast so he can definitely get around on the ball. And they're strong, too, though he's thin as a toothpick."

"He leads the club in home runs."

Mayo, silent, watched the kid take a couple more cuts.

"I bet he has twenty in another month."

"He can pound the ball. No doubt about it," Mayo conceded. "What concerns me, though, are his hands. They should be closer to his body so he can reach the low, inside pitch. Right now, his are too far away, and a good pitcher will see that and really bottle him up."

"I don't know, Mayo. He's pretty quick with the stick."

"He is, but it's much easier to swing inside out than it is to go outside in. You know that, skipper."

The manager frowned, spitting out a stream of tobacco juice. "There are so damn many things a person has to think about when he's up to bat it's a wonder he can make contact at all."

Mayo grinned. "The best hitting advice Ted Williams ever got, he claimed, was from Rogers Hornsby who told him 'Get a good ball to hit!'"

"Ain't that the truth."

*

"It must be close to ninety in the shade," a catcher complained as Mayo tossed him a rosin bag to dry off his slick hands so he could get a better grip on his bat.

"About that, yeah."

"I've been here almost six weeks and the heat just seems to get worse. I wonder if it'll ever cool off."

"Not likely. Not in this valley."

The catcher took a couple of easy swings, making sure he didn't lose his grip again. "You from around these parts, coach?"

He nodded. "I grew up in Seven Oaks."

"I've heard of it."

"It's a little ways east of here."

"I bet you're glad you got this assignment so you can see some of your family."

He didn't reply but watched Clete chop ground balls to some infielders.

"You still got some family there, don't you?"

"I don't know, to be honest. I haven't been back in a while."

"You going over there to see?"

He shrugged, wiping a bead of sweat from the tip of his nose with a thumbnail.

*

That evening, after dinner, Mayo started to drive back to his motel but on an impulse stayed on the highway and headed toward Seven Oaks. Oddly, he felt as if someone else were behind the wheel, and he was a passenger in his Jeep, unable to persuade the driver to turn around.

Half an hour later, still looming over the town like a dark cloud, appeared the old water tower that he and his cousin climbed one night on a mutual dare. And across it was the feed store, and farther on the bus depot and the library and in front of it the sullen Lincoln statue. Slowly he proceeded down the shaded street past the beauty parlor and Shell station and the bank and candy-striped candy store. There were a few places he didn't remember but otherwise the town remained pretty much as it was when he left to play for the Tigers.

Soon, as he knew he would, he saw Mullins Market, its weathered sign even larger than he remembered. At once, his heart banged against his ribs, causing his whole body to shudder for an instant. Tightly he gripped the steering wheel, not wanting to lose control of the Jeep as he drove past the market. He made a right at the corner and circled the block and approached the market again. Then, abruptly, he pulled into the nearly empty parking lot and turned off the engine, his hands still clutching the wheel.

He wondered if the Mullins family still owned the market. If so, he was sure he would remember them because, often at night, he still saw them glaring at him with the same fierce eyes at the inquest. Late one summer night, shortly after he signed with the Tigers, he and his cousin were tooling around in his uncle's El Dorado, racing through the back streets at the east end of town, when they struck and killed the Mullins' youngest daughter, April, who was out riding her bicycle. Neither of them saw her but knew they were at fault because they were going much too fast. Earnestly, at the inquest, he apologized to her family, but he knew from their eyes they didn't believe him. Maybe someone would tonight, he thought, climbing out of his Jeep.

In another moment, he was inside the market, and right away spotted a cashier who had the familiar round pale face of a Mullins. He took a deep breath, and as he approached her, he told himself to stay calm, not to fidget around, but to be absolutely still, just as he always instructed batters when they were at the plate.

The Dead Dance All Winter Long   Garrett Ashley

It is well known that in our world there can only be two absolutes: Death, and Inhalation. In order to be alive, one must breathe. But to be dead, simply put, is to cease to inhale, stop breathing, vanish, dry up, and blow away. Never before has a man continued to breath after his death. Nor has he ceased to breathe, while still alive.

By the time our story unfolds, it was Mr. and Mrs. Jonathan Carol's thirty-ninth anniversary. Mrs. Carol, being a small town lady of wondrous expectations, did not suspect the reason Mr. Carol had not made his way home yet as ill; her mind was on dinner (Mr. Carol would have agreed rather fondly that Mrs. Carol was a wonderful cook), and flowers, and blue skies, and the clouds. She was not your ordinary housewife, one might say. Mrs. Carol was not put down by the Way of the World or the Ordinaries which happened to occur right outside her kitchen window. Nothing had ever gone wrong with her life, and as far as the Carols could be concerned, they lived a perfectly happy existence. And she, unlike the other housewives on her street in little Lestenburough, was quite fond of the hour in which her husband was expected to arrive.

His work was at odds a half hour's drive away; by four-thirty, he would usually be getting off, and sometime around five he would pull into the garage. Mrs. Carol religiously sets the table before her husband could even reach the garage door. She was right fast in her art of being a house wife. Unfortunately this day, a Friday, resolved to be different than the rest. Dinner went cold.

At five thirty she began to worry. She thought to call the office, but decided against it, thinking that perhaps her husband had been delayed in some big-businessman like project. Mrs. Carol was not very keen on the lingo of business talk and business making, so she kept things simple, chose to be simple minded about her husband's work and his relations outside the home thereof. So she worried until the food was cold and the sound of Mr. Carol's car could be heard out in the garage, only an hour late. She went through the washroom to meet him, and begged him to tell her why he was late and if anything was the matter.

He shook his head, and smiled. "Lot of work. And I fell asleep at the desk. It was rough."

Mrs. Carol could not believe the sound of it. An Up man falling asleep on the job? Was this a joke? "Won't they fire you for sleeping? Were you being serious or just kidding around with me about sleeping?"

"I don't know if they'd just fire anyone for sleeping." His voice was sluggish and lazier than usual. "I've never thought about it." He leaned over and kissed Mrs. Carol; she was awfully short compared to his slender frame and stature. "How was your day?"

"It was all right, I guess," she said.

"Something smells good. What is it?"

"Don't you think it's your favorite, honey? Happy anniversary. Where are my flowers?"

Mr. Carol snapped his fingers. "Where's my mind? It's been slipping me all day." He made a walk back to the car.

"You forgot to pick me up flowers?" She hadn't meant to sound rude, but the thought of his forgetting something so traditional to their marriage bothered her.

"No, no. They're just here. Did you think I would forget?" He went back out to his car and brought her the dozen roses freshly bought. Perhaps they were the reason Mr. Carol was late. "Would you like to go out and eat tonight?"

Mrs. Carol flinched when her husband leaned over for another kiss. "But I just told you I cooked you your favorite! Yes, they're lovely. Thank you. But what are you talking about?"

"Oh nothing. I just thought you might want to do something different for our birthday."

Mrs. Carol let him pass into the kitchen without saying a word. It is true that Mr. Carol was acting quite strange; in fact, even his voice had changed. It somehow seemed a bit more hollow than it had the day before. Perhaps it was just her imagination playing tricks on her. The day, after all, had been an awfully cold, miserable, winter day. The mist and weather, it seemed, was the mortal enemy of a near perfect existence.

Mr. Carol was standing over the crock pot, his car keys still in hand. It looked as though maybe he were absorbing the contents of the pot, but upon further glance Mrs. Carol noticed that he was staring in a sort of morbid way at the food, rather than smelling it. "Is something wrong, Jonathan?"

It took a moment for his trance to break, and his eyes to fall back on Mrs. Carol. "Everything is fine, so far as I can tell. I can't wait to eat this. It looks delicious." He took a step back and walked to their bedroom. He usually changed into casual ware when home from work. This, perhaps, was the least unusual things he had done since arriving late.

"I thought you said you wanted to go out tonight?"

"No. I decided that since you cooked, it would be better for us to stay. Besides, it's pretty cold outside. I wouldn't want to get sick. Old people get sick. You know how it is when someone gets old."

"Yeah," said Mrs. Carol, an empty gloom rising slowly over her. "I think I do."

The evening passed rather quietly, and soon after dinner, and near bed time, and an unusually unsuccessful attempt at love making with Mr. Carol, they both went to bed. Mr. Carol didn't say a word after his head touched the pillow. Mrs. Carol, however, was awake most of the night, troubled about her husband in too many ways to accept. She tried to listen to his breathing. It seemed normal. Rather quick, actually, but nothing too unusual to get a start out of. She listened, and listened, and listened, until she fell asleep herself.

The next morning, she found him lying awake with his eyes up on the ceiling. "You 'right, Mr. Carol?"

"'malright," he said with that odd, dreamy, lazy voice. "I'm afraid I may be late for work."

"It's Saturday," she said. "Are you sure you're alright?"

Jonathan Carol's eyes still focused hard on the ceiling. Once or twice Mrs. Carol looked up to see what he saw. Just little shapes in the textures of white paint, like shapes of animals and objects in the clouds. "I didn't know it was Saturday," he said. "I think I'll just lie here then, if it's alright. I don't mean to be a bother."

"No bother honey," she said, rubbing Mr. Carol's forehead like she was checking his temperature. "I'll stay here with you. Don't mind getting a bit extra sleep if I can..." She looked up at the alarm clock. "It's too early for a Saturday anyway."

"I don't mind being alone," said Mr. Carol.

Mrs. Carol roused herself from the covers. "You want me to go somewhere else?"

"It doesn't matter," he said. "I didn't get much sleep last night."

"You were awake?"

"Yes. I was thinking about work today."

Mrs. Carol stepped out of bed. Her night gown was in a wad at first; she fixed it quickly, like Mr. Carol was a stranger and had no business being in the room with her while she was so unwound. "I'll leave you to it, then," she said. She went to the kitchen, started coffee, and tried hard not to cry.

At nine-thirty, she went to check on Mr. Carol. He was up now; the bathroom door was shut. She could hear him brushing his teeth. Soon after, she could hear water running in the shower. She picked up the kitchen phone and dialed her sister's number. A woman answered on the other side, "Hello?"

"It's me," said Mrs. Carol. "I'm sorry to call so early. How are you and Luther?"

"We're fine. What time is it?"

"Early, I know," she said again. "I'm just having a problem—well I don't know if it's a problem or not, but I was a little worried about Jonathan."

"I've always been worried about Jonathan," said the voice on the other side.

"He's just been acting really strange since he got in yesterday evening," said Mrs. Carol. "I was just wondering if you knew anything about Luther's Father?"

"He died before we married."

"Well, I know," said Mrs. Carol, "But I know Luther talked a lot about his father's Alzheimer's. What's that kind of thing like?"

"I think Jonathan's a little too young for it," said the voice on the other side.

"I don't know," said Mrs. Carol. "May be a little too early to tell, anyway. But what kind of things did Luther's Father do?"

"Well, nothing too interesting," said the voice. "He did tell me this one really funny story about how his daddy would pee in the gas heater, right there in a den full of people. I didn't tell him I thought it was funny, I just figured he already knew it, and might have already had a laugh about it, but that's not the kind of thing you want to go on about, especially when the man you're laughing at's dead, and he's your husband's daddy…"

"That doesn't sound good at all," said Mrs. Carol. "So you don't think I should call Dr. Beck just yet? That's all I wanted to know. Jonathan was staring at the ceiling all night. He said he didn't get any sleep."

"Don't call just yet. Give it a little time. If he does anything weird, give me a call and we'll both have a laugh. Remember I'm right here!"

By Wednesday, when the cold had thickened and the pounding wind and rain coming on and going off had become unbearable, Mrs. Carol had still not felt it absolutely necessary to call and speak with Dr. Beck about her husband. Perhaps he had been acting odd, talking about work on mornings when he'd not be inclined to go in—Sunday had been the same as the day before—but on the days he did work, he talked about working, likewise; therefore it deemed less odd than the weekend prior. It was not until the late afternoon that she received a phone call from an unusual voice, a man, someone Mrs. Carol hardly recognized as a fellow employee of Jonathan Carol.

"Hello?" she answered. It was not very common that her voice answer with such hostility, but her husband had proven late again, and for the sixth day now she had been a bit more worried than the last.

"Hello?" said the voice on the other side. "Is this Mrs. Carol?"

"Speaking."

"Oh, hmm, I was just wondering if Jonathan had made it home alright. He's been a bit ill lately, I was just wondering how he's been doing at home?"

"Who wants to know?"

"Mr. Kenner," he said. "He's been sleeping a lot at the office. Just letting his head fall onto his desk face flat. I haven't seen behavior like that from 'em before. Have you noticed anything? Why's he not getting any sleep at home?"

"Can't say that's any of your business why," she said. "But I'll take note of it. He's been a little unusual, lately, yes. Thank you. If it goes on I'm going to call a doctor. I'm afraid he may have a touch of Alzheimer's.

"I doubt it, given his age. Tell him to take the rest of the week off. I hate seeing him like this; he needs a break, anyway. Both of you do."

Mrs. Carol thanked Mr. Kenner again, and said goodbye. She wondered what he meant by his last statement; perhaps he thought that she had been behaving the same way—that being a house wife made you tired, or behave oddly, or both; this, in turn, made her assume Mr. Kenner was blaming her for her husband's behavior. Mrs. Carol had never been so assuming of anyone!

This time running two hours late, Jonathan Carol trudged in, his eyes fixed on the floor as he walked. Though his body seemed to misstep, his legs like rubber, he glided across the floor in a mystic fashion. He did not speak to Mrs. Carol, just went to the den to sit in the overstuffed chair, and stare at the blank television screen.

She sat on the sofa nearby, not daring to be any closer. "I heard you fell asleep at work," she said. "Do I need to get you some help?"

"Help?" he said. He looked up at her, his face blank as a pale slate. "Thank you. But I have a feeling everything is going to be just fine."

Mrs. Carol imagined herself asking him what was the matter with his voice, then continued aloud as though she had actually inquired: "And what do you mean by 'just fine?' I'm trying to tell you you're not looking and actin' right, don't you know? I'm scared!"

Mr. Carol's glare stayed fixed on the blank television screen. It was an empty shell, and so were his eyes. They were the deepest of pits, nothing like Mrs. Carol had ever seen in her dear, sweet husband. "You shouldn't be scared," he said. "Everything is going to be alright."

Mrs. Carol cooked a small meal for them to eat, but her husband passed on his portion. It was starting to look as though he had passed on many. The next day was the same. Despite Mr. Kenner's suggesting that Jonathan stay away from work for the remainder of the week, he got up in the morning and left anyway. He came in a bit late—not quite as late as the day before—skipped a meal, then a conversation, and went to bed. Mrs. Carol had been sleeping on the couch since Tuesday.

Friday was perhaps the most unusual day of the transformation. Mr. Carol was no less than three hours late coming home, when a different car pulled into the driveway. A knock at the front door always means bad news, especially when a loved one is away for so long. Three hours is a lifetime for a small town woman like Mrs. Carol. She opened the door to an unfamiliar face. The man didn't smile, nor did he look in any way pleased to see her: "Can I help you?" she asked.

"I'm Mr. Kenner," said the man. A glum look on his face spoke ill of Jonathan Carol. "Are you doing well this evening, Mrs. Carol?"

"I'm fine," she said. "But where is my husband? What's the matter?"

"Well," said Mr. Kenner. He looked slightly nervous about what he was about to say. "We had an ambulance come and get him. He fell asleep again, and we couldn't wake him up."

Mrs. Carol's insides went numb.

"He did eventually come around. We asked if he needed a doctor..."

"You hadn't already called one?"

"Well, no," he said. "We'd gotten so used to him acting strange and sleeping, we just figured he was an awful lot more tuckered out than usual. Like I said, we asked if he needed a doctor. We *insisted*, actually."

"Did he tell you it'd be alright?"

"He said *Everything* would be alright. Don't know what he was getting at. But a few minutes later he went to the restroom, and we heard a great deal of screamin' and fightin.' I went to check... I called the hospital and an ambulance came to pick him up. He's alright now. I figured I'd pick you up and bring you out there; maybe you can talk to a doctor before they send him home. It's all just happened; I would have called sooner..."

"It's fine, really, it is." She reassured Mr. Kenner, nervous as he was, and had him take her to the hospital, where she would find him sitting in a waiting room as though he had not even seen a doctor. He was looking quite hollow, and barely noticed his wife as she came in and took a seat next to him.

"Mr. Kenner brought me up, said you were doing just fine," she said to him. He was cold. Not fine. She knew her husband better than that. "Where's your doctor?"

It was a while before she could speak to Dr. Beck. He was a small man, much shorter than Mrs. Carol, with buzzed grey hair and a curly little mustache like a magician. She didn't like him, even before he spoke. He tried, and may have succeeded, to convince Mrs. Carol that Jonathan did not have Alzheimer's. "Possibly, if anything," he said, "anger issues. He'd broken all the mirrors in the restroom where he works. I can prescribe him medication, or find him a psychologist. If it's a domestic issue, it's treatable. Otherwise, I can't say that anything's wrong with Jonathan Carol at all."

Dr. Beck made Mrs. Carol so angry, she swore that if she ever became sick to the point of death in need of medical attention, she would certainly rather stay home and die.

Mr. Carol did not get any better; nor did he return to work the week after. Mr. Kenner promised that if the couple needed anything, he would be more than happy to help. Mrs. Carol began to lose weight; she's stopped eating dinner, being so used to Mr. Carol passing on meals. But then, one day, he stopped eating altogether. He barely spoke. When he did speak, his voice frightened Mrs. Carol. "Do not worry," he would say, "Everything will be alright." His voice had changed, his grammar, the way he looked at Mrs. Carol when he spoke. Sometimes, he didn't look at all.

She missed the way Mr. Carol would bring her flowers from time to time. Their recent anniversary had been the last time; this thought stayed with her mind, usually as she tried to fall asleep at night. It was hurting her, having to sleep in a different place, away from her darling, laughing, humble husband. She could not help but to be afraid of him. But it hurt so terribly bad, that one night she decided to go back to sleep with him. "I love you, Mr. Carol," she said. "I love you too," he replied with a dreamy, uneasy voice. She felt calm again, but his body was so cold, she could not be too near him. He moved around a lot in his sleep. She thought he must have been sleeping... he had not been to work, and had not fallen asleep any during the day.

She wondered about what Dr. Beck said about domestic issues. Was she a bad wife? Was it her fault that Mr. Carol was acting so strange? Then she thought about the last time he had brought her flowers again. Not necessarily the fact that he had remembered to buy them or that he had been sweet enough to do so, but simply that he had forgotten them in the car, and given them to her so casually as though it didn't really matter at all.

Mr. Carol sat up in bed, and remained still thereafter. Mrs. Carol watched him; perhaps he was dreaming. His eyes were focused on something across the way. The mirror on the dresser; it was too large not to see. Mr. Carol seemed empty again, but his wife tried hard to ignore it. It couldn't be domestic issues. Something was certainly the matter. His top half lowered slowly, silently to the bed and his head touched the pillow and rested as it had done so before. A good while into the night, just before Mrs. Carol could fall asleep, he threw himself up again, his voice rattled a bit like he was trying to talk. This startled Mrs. Carol; she had herself as far away from him on her side of the bed as she could be. If she left the covers, would he notice?

Or would he attack her?

Or would he say anything at all?

When he did finally lie back down, Mrs. Carol left the bed, and returned to the den to sleep once again. The next morning, she went to check on him in the bedroom. The mirror on the dresser had been taken apart and was resting reflection-down against the wall behind the bed's headboard. She could hear him brushing his teeth in the bathroom; he was making odd, mechanical strokes, quick, organized. She didn't go in to see him. After the night before, she wondered whether it would be wise to speak with him at all.

Another week ended, another began. So the days went by in pain, and Mrs. Carol's darling, laughing, humble husband grew stranger by the hour. He would not allow her to replace the mirrors in the house. He barely had to demand their absence; a whisper or too was enough to convince Mrs. Carol to leave them be. "They make me think a lot," he said to her in that hollow, misty voice. "I have been thinking a lot. Do people have souls?"

Mrs. Carol could feel her face flush red. They were the church going type (though neither of the two had been in ages), and Mr. Carol was not the sort to ask such a ridiculous question. "Yeah," she said. "I think they do."

"Where do they go?"

This was the most he had said in several days. It frightened Mrs. Carol a little to hear his words. "I guess they go to heaven. Sometimes they don't, but I don't think you need to worry about that."

Mr. Carol gave a nod, and stared into the nothingness of space. Over the next several days Mrs. Carol thought to call back

Dr. Beck. She considered a psychologist, but what with the fact that Mr. Carol was out of work with hardly a way to pay the bills, they had better just not go on with such nonsense. Then she thought about calling a priest. Would he tell her that her husband was possessed? Or would he tell her that Jonathan Carol was an empty shell? The face is the window to the soul. When Mrs. Carol looked into her husband's eyes, she saw that the windows were empty. His body was an empty, breathing, soulless machine. A practical dead man, walking through the wintertime. She would not like being told that. But at long last, it wouldn't matter. Nobody would come. There was no use in even considering it.

His began to turn pale. Then it turned gray. Mrs. Carol didn't consider his malnutrition to be the cause. It was something else, something deep, dark, unexplainable. His eyes sunk into his head. Around them, his skin pulled tight, not like a corpse, but like a fine young man lying cold in a funeral parlor. One night, just before getting off to bed, he said to her: "I'm afraid." His voice was empty, yet so childlike that it brought Mrs. Carol to tears. "Don't leave me alone."

"I won't," she said, and went to bed with him. All the night she could feel him breathing, watching the little textures in the ceiling covered in shadow. He must have been looking for shapes in the clouds, hoping to find something good, beautiful enough to endure a smile.

He threw himself upright, just as he had done before; he was looking at the blank wall where the mirror had once existed. Some while later, he stood up and walked quietly to the bathroom. Mrs. Carol tried to watch him in the darkness. He seemed to just stand there, still as a board, watching back. The more uneasy Mrs. Carol felt, the more she wanted to flee the room. Run, and never come back. She wasn't Mrs. Carol anymore, and Jonathan Carol was not her husband. She reached for the lamp, and let the light flow in.

He gave a cry of pain, lifted his arms to his eyes to deflect the light. He fell backward over a pair of slippers; his skull crashed against the toilet lid, made a loud, cracking sound. His feet kicked and twisted, then his hands flew up along with his torso, like he was trying to get up. Trying to dance his way up, as though nothing had ever destroyed him in the first place.

Then he managed to fling himself up, never making a sound, expect for the things his dancing arms smashed wildly against. Mrs. Carol saw that his eyes had rolled behind his head, the whites were bloodshot. He danced. Mrs. Carol screamed. Mr. Carol, stopping his feet, twirled around then fell to his knees. He flung his head and torso back as though crying out to God for mercy. But no sound came out of his mouth. His arms danced. Then he didn't move.

At the funeral, Mr. Kenner sat with Ms. Carol. He had been good to her, and though she still had not gotten over her husband's strange goodbye, appreciated with the warmness of Mr. Kenner's sympathy. "It was good to meet your children," he said to her. "I didn't even know their names. Jonathan always talked about them. But I'm never really good with names."

Ms. Carol found it hard to pay attention to anything Mr. Kenner said. She'd just as well not have any children. "What do you think it means to die?" she asked.

Mr. Kenner shook his head. He wasn't very good with these things, and had not expected it. "I don't think it means anything to die, unless you're a religious person. I guess it means more to be alive than anything. I don't really know. Not even sure about what it means to be alive, if you want to know the truth."

"He asked me if people have souls," she said. "It was the worst question anyone's ever asked me. I kind of started to wonder that myself over the past few weeks."

"What do you think?"

Ms. Carol whispered so that only she and Mr. Kenner could understand. "I think they do," she said. "Jonathan did. You should have seen him die. It was the worst thing I've ever seen in my life."

"You don't have to think of that," said Mr. Kenner. "It was an accident, that's all."

"It was going to be our thirty-ninth anniversary," she said, no longer paying attention to the man sitting inches away from her. "Something happened to him that day. Something I'll never be able to explain. I wonder if it's ever happened to anyone else."

      Mr. Kenner put his arm around Ms. Carol. She looked over at her husband's body. Jonathan Carol was himself again; it looked as though he were smiling. His skin color had returned, though he was the same size as the day he stopped moving. She imagined him smiling at her. Then she imagined him jumping up and out of the coffin, dancing, twirling, twisting, never crying out, never saying goodbye, never making an effort to sound at all. Then she remembered that the dead don't dance. They can't breathe, so they don't dance. "Do you think he knew?" she said.

Scarecrow Fort   Ron D'Alena

I'm alone in the waiting room. Then Old Lady comes in, sits next me. Rhinestone flower pinned to her knitted sweater twinkles yellow-pink under fluorescent lights. It would look darling on the bamboo-color turtleneck I am wearing.

Old Lady coughs and coughs. Each eye a little slit in her wrinkled face. She begins talking about all sorts of things – the rain, the mice in her in kitchen pantry, how there was nothing good to read anymore. Suddenly she slides to the edge of her metal chair and leans into me and asks, When was your first cigarette?

You mean my very, very first?

Yes, how did all this happen?

I hesitate and pull my winter coat tighter about my shoulders. I say, It was 1972, shortly after my eleventh birthday. On the way home from school, me and Debbie Campari stopped at the 7-Eleven to get a Pepsi. Jimmy Hill was there, leaning against the store siding, talking with Amy Fong and Matt Nelson. Debbie giggled. She was the only person in the entire world who knew of my crush on Jimmy.

When I came out of the store Jimmy said, Hi Susan. His breath was red licorice. His eyes were chestnuts. His hair was a mess of dry straw.

I said, Hi.

Debbie giggled.

Jimmy pushed heavy hands through tangled hair. He said, We're going to Scarecrow Fort. You want to come along?

I stood with the Pepsi bottle cold in my hand, pretending to give real consideration to the offer. The idea of going to Scarecrow Fort was silly. Popular kids went there. Me and Debbie were bookworms.

Debbie squinted at me. I knew what she was thinking: I didn't have to get home; Widow Sears (the woman from our church caring for me while my parents were vacationing in Florida) would think nothing of me being late.

I said, I can't. I've got to get home.

Jimmy said, That's too bad.

Then Debbie, Debbie, Debbie - Debbie said, I'll go. Can I go?

Sure, you can.

They turned toward the sidewalk and walked away – Debbie looking over her shoulder, grinning at me. Then an inescapable truth struck me. If ever I was going to take liberties, it had to be now, while my parents were away.

I ran down the sloping parking lot and locked arms at the elbow with the girl I'd known since kindergarten. We giggled and when a school bus passed by we unlocked our arms and waved to the unfortunate kids who had no choice but to go home. Seeing those kids trapped behind the little square windows made me thank God my parents were on vacation.

The afternoon air: warm and heavy with the mellow scent of apricot blossoms from the surrounding orchards. As we walked, I felt older, like a lazy teenager. And when Amy Fong began to hum I became so happy that I almost wept.

We lolled in front of a Shell filling station. Jimmy went into the garage where his older brother worked as a mechanic. They talked. Then Jimmy's brother went over to an old Pontiac and Jimmy went over to the cigarette machine next to the office door. He dropped a few coins into the slot, pulled a lever, reached his over-sized hand into the metal tray, withdrew a pack of Marlboros. I took a deep breath. I was going to Scarecrow Fort!

We walked past Freddy's Market, a corner grocery – people going in, coming out, smiling at us, never suspecting the mischief in our hearts. We walked through a neighborhood with no sidewalk, no streetlights, lined with red oaks. Jimmy picked up a rock and threw it at a big old tabby sunning himself next to a tomato garden.

At the end of the street, where the neighborhood stopped, was a vacant lot overgrown with blackberry bushes. Jimmy led us to the center of the lot, to the largest thicket of all. He pointed to a tunnel cut into this thicket.

We crawled and crawled, scraping our knees, scuffing our shoes, coming at last to a hollowed out area: eight-feet square, littered with a million crushed cigarette butts, shaded from the golden sunshine by vines with five leaf clusters and small white flowers. And there in the center of the clearing was Mrs. Fisher's old Halloween scarecrow – ragged, missing for three years.

Hurrah, Scarecrow Fort!

Jimmy ripped the cellophane from the pack, threw it on the ground, lit a cigarette. And then, using the end of his cigarette, he lit a cigarette for each of us. I put the cigarette between nervous lips. Smoke curled up, killed the air in my nose, watered my eyes. Amy Fong gestured to me, told me I was doing it wrong, told me I had to inhale everything into my lungs.

I coughed for five minutes.

Everyone laughed – seems Jimmy was the only one that ever inhaled.

We sat on the ground, bare feet pushed into warm dirt, surrounded by cigarette butts and cellophane and ants, talking about the movies, smoking cigarettes like they do on television.

At the end of it all, Jimmy was prepared for cigarette breath, surprising us with a red licorice rope pulled from his jacket pocket. That's why everyone trusted Jimmy – because of his foresight.

That night I trembled like a scared criminal – my head was wrong, my heart was black, my soul was that of an old crow. But in my sleep angels purged me of my sin. By morning, I felt good enough to sneak three cigarettes from the purse of Widow Sears without her ever knowing.

Old Lady coughs and coughs. She leans into the faded cushion of her chair and says, That's quite an account of things, Susan. Would you like to hear about my first time?

The receptionist calls my name.

I'm sorry, I say, maybe you can tell me on another visit.

As I move across the waiting room, I look over my left shoulder at Old Lady. We smile to one another. Then I stifle a cough with the back of my hand and enter a hallway dim with fluorescent lighting.

Also appears in Cause & Effect Magazine

"What do you mean? You've never been to church?" Natalie's eyes widened.

Tanya shook her head.

"Never ever? Don't you believe in Jesus?"

"Uhhh..." Tanya said. "I don't know."

"Everyone should believe in Jesus. He died for our sins."

"Okay." Tanya didn't know what to say. She didn't believe or disbelieve, it just never came up before.

They were playing Go Fish at recess when the subject came up. Natalie pulled out another pair. "You should totally come with me. It's really fun. We sing songs, we learn about Jesus. You do know who Jesus is, right?"

"Yeah," Tanya said.

"And we play on the playground afterwards. You know, my dad's the preacher."

"Really?" Tanya said, "Like the lead guy?"

"Yeah. In fact, that's why we moved down here. And then afterwards, we can go play in the youth room. It's got this big plasma TV with Nintendo. My dad got it special."

"When is it?"

"It's Sunday. It's <u>always</u> Sunday. At nine-thirty. You can sit by me, and then afterwards I can get my dad to take us to Dairy Queen."

"Really?" Tanya said as she put down her pair of queens. "I'll have to ask my parents."

"You can bring them along. Maybe they want to go to church too."

"I don't think they're religious."

"Don't you know? Don't they say grace before dinner or make you pray before bed?"

"No," Tanya said. "Is that what you do?"

"Yeah, that's what every family does."

"I was adopted when I was a baby," Tanya said. She'd always known she was adopted, but it didn't bother her. She had a mom and a dad that made sure she got breakfast in the morning, helped her with her homework, and read her a story before bed. "Would that be why?"

"No," Natalie mocked. "Everyone needs to go to church, at least once in a while, and ours is the coolest. It's only an hour. I bet if you tell them you want to go, they'll go."

"Do you think that will work?"

"Pssh," she scoffed. "They can't say no. Not unless they want to burn in Hell. Just tell them you want to see your friends."

Tanya nodded. "Okay, I'll ask them."

#

That evening, as her mom put her plate in front of her, Tanya said, "Mom, can we go with Natalie to church on Sunday?"

Tanya's mom froze, the hand still on her plate. She glanced at her husband, Victor. "What was that, dear?" she said.

"I want us to go to church with Natalie. She said church is really fun. And I thought it would be better if we could all go."

"Natalie's that new girl, right? From Massachusetts?" her father asked.

They exchanged another look. Tanya's mom, Rose, took her seat at the table. "Errr, dear, I don't think that's such a good idea."

"Why not?"

Her mom bit her lip, "Ummm..."

"Can Natalie just pick you up?" her dad said.

"I don't think so," she said after a thought. "Her dad's the preacher so I bet they have to be there extra early. Besides it sounds fun. We never do anything on Sunday mornings anyway."

Rose and Victor stared at each other. Tanya didn't know why they were taking so long to make up their minds. This was a no-brainer.

"I think we have to..." her mom said. "Uh... clean the house."

"Clean the house?" Tanya said. "We cleaned it last week."

Victor put his hand on his wife's shoulder. "Guess she was going to find out sometime."

Rose nodded solemnly. "Honey?" she said to Tanya, "We need to tell you something."

Tanya's eyes widened and her heart beat faster.

"I didn't really want you to find out like this. But, you'll need to know some time."

Her dad said, "This is something we never told you before. We're vampires."

Tanya's eyes had been watering, ready to cry. Now she furrowed her brows. "Huh?"

"We're vampires," her dad repeated. "We can't go inside a church."

She had no idea how to take that as anything but a joke. Tanya expected them to shout 'just kidding!'. But they remained stoic and waited for a response from her. "You're not kidding."

"I wish I was, honey," Rose said.

"You are not vampires," Tanya laughed.

"Yes, honey, we are."

"Then why don't you have fangs?" Tanya pointed to their mouths.

"They're retractable, like a snake. They can fold in."

Tanya smirked. "Show me."

Rose and Victor looked at each other again. Her mom opened her mouth like she was going to take a bite from an apple.

Her two front canines descended an inch from her upper jaw.

Tanya shoved away from the table, upsetting her chair and falling on her tailbone. Heedless of the pain, she scrambled up and backed away.

Her parents held up their hands. "Tanya, Tanya, it's okay, it's okay. We're not going to hurt you."

All she could see were the fangs in her mom's mouth, sticking out like a crocodile's.

"How did you do that? That's not real," Tanya said.

"Yes, it is real, I'm afraid," Rose said.

"Don't worry, honey," her dad said. "We still love you. We're still the same people that raised you."

She stopped backing away when she saw their eyes. There was no malice in them. They still looked like her parents, but pointier.

"You're really vampires," Tanya said.

"Yes."

"Do you drink blood?"

"Well, yes. That's kind of the core part of being a vampire," Victor said.

"Human blood?"

"Yes. That's the only kind we can have," Rose said.

"But you eat regular food!" She pointed to the plates of food in front of them.

"We can eat regular food, but it doesn't give us all the nutrients that we need," Victor said. "It's like another food group for us. Did you learn about the four food groups in school?"

"There's five now, dear," Rose said.

Tanya ignored the question. "You don't... kill people for it?"

"Oh, no. We buy it from a blood bank. We have someone deliver it and keep it in the freezer in our room," Victor said.

"But I've never seen you drink blood."

"We drink it when you're sleeping. We don't need much per day."

"Is that why your room is in the basement? Do you sleep in coffins?"

"No, but we do need to sleep on the dirt of our homeland every night," Rose said.

"Way back in the past, we used to be like the vampires you see on TV, but we're not anymore. We got tired of that," Victor said.

"Always running away, always hiding." Rose looked at her husband. "I guess we're still hiding, somewhat. But now at least we're not being pursued."

"Did you kill people?"

Her father sighed. "Yes, I'm afraid so. But it was for their blood. We needed it to live. Now with modern technology, we don't need to do that, so we gave it up. Not everyone did."

"Am I a vampire?"

"No. Remember, you were adopted," Victor said.

"Are you going to make me a vampire?"

They laughed. "Oh, lord, no. No, of course not."

Rose joked, "You're the only one of us that can go outside."

"Then why did you adopt me?" Tanya asked. She thought of being fattened up like in Hansel & Gretel.

"Because we wanted to be a family. We've been together for," she thought, "Decades, at least. We wanted something new. And vampires can't, um," she tried to think of the appropriate word, "Have children on their own."

"What? Like with fertility drugs?"

"No, I mean. Well-"

Victor interrupted. "Being a vampire is part disease, part magic, part possession. So our bodies don't work the same. That means we can't have children like normal."

"Oh," Tanya said. She still didn't understand, but decided to let it go. "How long have you been... not vampiring?"

"Let's see," Rose said, "Sixty years ago, I think. That's when the blood bank opened."

Victor nodded. "Back then we were living in run-down buildings, or underground. There's nothing really great about being a vampire, except for the immortality. But that has its good and bad too."

"Uh-huh," Tanya said. "I guess this explains why you always went to the evening parent-teacher conferences."

They nodded. "Are you okay with this?" Victor said.

Tanya scratched her head, "I don't know... I mean... I don't know."

"You're still our daughter," her mom said, "And we still love you and we would never do anything to hurt you. I'm sorry this came up like it did, but we didn't know how you would react."

"And please don't tell anyone what we are," Victor said. "Just because we don't want someone snooping around, or risk being run out of town."

"They probably won't believe you, but they might get scared and try to hurt us," Rose added.

Tanya kept staring at the ground. She couldn't look at them.

"Honey, will you please come and finish your dinner?" Rose said.

Tanya rubbed the back of her neck and, failing to come up with a good excuse, sat back down.

#

Tanya didn't sleep that night. She couldn't stop going over everything in her life that proved her parents were vampires--everything she should have noticed before. Their skin was pale. They only went outside in the evening. All the windows were UV tinted.

Their master bedroom had a deadbolt and she was forbidden from going in there. She thought it was because they wanted their private time. No, they just wanted to drink their blood in peace.

They didn't walk her out to the bus on her first day of kindergarten, like the other kids. They didn't go to the school's open house. And although they looked younger than parents she saw on TV, they acted old--old hairstyles, old clothes. They had been alive for decades. Well, not alive, but around.

Tanya didn't know much about vampires. The only real exposure she had was <u>Scooby-Doo</u> and <u>Casper</u> cartoons. But her parents were real vampires, like in the advertisements for R-rated movies she would never see in a million years. The ones that bit you on the neck, and made blood drip down your skin...

Tanya whimpered. Tears ran down her nose. She imagined her parents lurking in a dark alley and grabbing some unsuspecting passerby. They held him against the wall as her dad plunged his fangs into his leg, and her mom sunk into his neck. And they feasted while he flailed his arms, helpless and dying.

They could be doing that now. They could be creeping into her room. She imagined her door creaking open, revealing two long shadows in the sickly yellow light. Long gangly fingers reached for her.

She pulled the covers over her head and cried.

#

"Oh, honey, you look awful," her dad said in the morning.

"I... didn't sleep," Tanya said.

Victor sipped his coffee. Or maybe it was warm blood, or coffee mixed with blood. "I'm sorry. I guess I should've figured that."

Rose knelt down and felt Tanya's face. "Do you feel okay? Do you want to stay home today?"

Any kid with half a brain would have jumped at an opportunity for a day off. But Tanya thought of the alternative-- all day in a house of vampires. "No, I'm fine. I can go."

"You sure? You can stay home if you want."

"I'm fine, really."

"Okay, I made you some pancakes."

"Pancakes?" Her eyes brightened.

"You probably had a pretty rough day yesterday. I promise it'll get easier as you go on."

"You'll get used to it, I hope," her father said. "We have."

"How long have you been... you know?"

Victor looked up at the ceiling. "Let's see. I turned in 1919. I remember it was the flu epidemic."

"1857 for me," Rose said.

"So you're the older one?" Tanya pointed. "That's kinda funny."

Her mom smiled as she put down the plate of pancakes. "I guess it is."

Tanya ate her breakfast, but kept an eye on her parents. The thought of being poisoned crossed her mind, but that didn't make sense. For one thing, vampires didn't poison, and second, why would they poison her now, when they could have done that ages ago?

"Oh, the bus is almost here," her mom said. "Hurry up."

95

Tanya checked the clock and saw she was right. She jumped off the chair and grabbed her backpack. Her mother escorted her to the door and bent down to give her a kiss.

The image of her mother's teeth growing like daggers sprung to mind. Tanya pulled her head back. Her mother paused, obviously hurt.

But she was just trying to be a good mom. She was telling the truth last night--nothing had really changed. Tanya offered her cheek again, and her mom kissed it.

"Have a good day," she said.

#

Tanya muddled through the day on autopilot--caused by both the lack of sleep and the situation.

At recess she sat under the shade of a tree, too tired to play. She watched the other kids and wondered if things would ever be normal again.

A small scab on her knee caught her eye, from when she bumped into the coffee table a week ago. She picked the crusty brown mass away with her fingernail. A small dome of bright red blood oozed out. Blood just like her parents drank.

She wiped it away, leaving a red streak on her knee. She put her finger in her mouth. It didn't taste like anything.

Natalie came up to her, along with their friend Patty. "Hey, Tanya," Natalie said. "Why aren't you playing?"

"I don't know. I don't feel good," Tanya said.

"Oh, that's too bad," Patty said.

"Did you ask your parents about church?" Natalie said.

"Uh, yeah." Tanya drew in the dirt with a twig.

"Yeah? And?"

"They can't come."

Natalie made a pouty face. "Ohhh, why not?"

"Nothing."

"Nothing?" Natalie said, "What do you mean 'nothing'?"

"Nothing. I mean, they can't go to church."

Patty said, "Why? Are they sick?"

"No," Natalie growled, "That's stupid. How would they know they're going to be sick? Are they Satanists?" Natalie asked.

"No, not really," Tanya replied. "They just can't go, ever."

"'Not really'? What does that mean? They can't ever go to church? What, are they vampires or something?"

Tanya tilted her head back and forth. "Yeah, kinda."

At first they said nothing. Patty snickered. Natalie's jaw dropped. "Yeah, right," she said, "Are you serious?"

Tanya nodded, not making eye contact.

"They're not vampires. How do they go out?" Natalie said.

"They only go out at night," Tanya said. "That's the way it's always been. Our windows are those special shaded kind. So there's no sunlight."

"Don't they have jobs?" Natalie said.

"No, they don't need to. They have inherited money, I guess. I think they sleep during the day when I'm at school."

Natalie turned to Patty. "Is she being serious?"

Patty shrugged. "I've never seen her parents. Or been in her house."

Natalie asked Tanya, "Are you serious? Your parents are really vampires? Like 'vampire' vampires?"

Tanya nodded again. "My mom showed me her teeth. They literally grew out of her mouth like this." She held up her fingers to the upper part of her mouth and mimed the incisors moving down. "And they drink blood. They get it from a blood bank."

"Oh my gosh," Natalie said, "Have you ever seen them drink blood?"

"No. They don't drink it in front of me." Tanya shook her head. "I think they do it at night. They keep their bedroom door locked."

Natalie said, "If they're real, you have to kill them."

"What?" Tanya looked up with horror.

Natalie nodded. "They're vampires, aren't they? Vampires are evil. You have to kill them."

"I can't kill them, they're my parents."

"They're not your real parents. They adopted you, remember?" Tanya had to concede that point and nodded. "Vampires can't raise a family. They're evil things."

"They're not evil anymore, they said."

"You're going to believe them? Vampires always tell the truth?"

Patty said, "What if she just runs away?"

"You can't let vampires keep on living," Natalie said, "What if they kill someone?"

"They said they don't do that anymore," Tanya said.

"But they did. And what's to stop them from doing it again?"

Patty said, "Maybe they're nice. My mom's always reading books where girls fall in love with vampires."

Natalie stuck out her chin. "Patty, these aren't like aliens, where some are good and some are bad. They're monsters. They drink people's blood."

Tanya thought back to the images of last night--of her parents' mouths dug deep into the flesh of their victim, eyes red with evil.

"But if I kill them, what's going to happen to me?" Tanya asked.

"Well, do you have any relatives?"

Tanya shook her head. "I'm adopted, and I don't have any uncles or anything like that."

"Then they'll probably put you in a foster home."

Tanya's eyes watered.

"But it's better than living with vampires," Natalie amended.

"How do you kill a vampire?" Patty asked.

"A stake through the heart," Natalie said without hesitation. "When they're sleeping."

"I can't do that," Tanya said. "I can't stab someone."

"It's the only way. It's how they always do it."

Patty interjected, "How is she going to do that if her parents lock their door?"

"Okay, okay," Natalie said, "There's other things. There's garlic."

"We don't have garlic in our house," Tanya said.

"Well, obviously," Natalie said, "You'd have to get it from somebody. I have garlic at my house. Or there's crosses. You can make a cross out of anything."

"Holy water," Patty suggested.

"Oh, perfect," Natalie said. "I can get some from my dad. He's a preacher."

"We know," Patty said.

"What am I supposed to do with the holy water?" Tanya said.

"Throw it on them," Natalie said.

"But that won't kill them," Patty said. "It'll just burn them. But I saw on TV where a vampire drank it, and that killed him."

"Yeah, yeah. Make them drink it," Natalie said as if she'd thought of it.

"What am I supposed to do?" Tanya said, "Just hand them some random water and say 'hey, drink this'."

"No, silly, put it in their food."

Tanya tried to think of a problem with that, but couldn't.

"Does it stay holy water if you put it in food?" Patty asked.

"I guess so. I don't see why not. If it doesn't work, they still won't know."

Tanya pleaded, "I can't kill my parents. I can't kill anyone."

Natalie frowned. "If you don't, I'm going to tell someone. We can't have vampires on the streets in this town."

Patty sneered, "Who are you going to tell? Who would believe you?"

"We believe her. And I'd tell my dad. He'd do something about it, I know."

Tanya thought back to the cartoons and movies. There was always some sort of priest or concerned mother who got the town up in arms. She imagined a mob with torches and guns at her front door.

"You can't do that," Tanya said. "The police won't let you."

"They're vampires. They don't deserve to live. Either you kill them, or I'll get someone else to do it. You can stay at my house afterwards. And if it doesn't affect them, you'll know they aren't vampires. Now are you going to take the holy water or not?"

Tanya looked away, then nodded.

"Good, I'll get you some tomorrow."

#

When Tanya got home from school, she didn't talk to her parents much. She mostly watched TV--more than her parents would usually let her. But all the time, she was keeping a close eye on them--seeing if they exhibited any of the murderous vampire traits.

Her mother vacuumed and dusted the upstairs. Her father read in the kitchen for a while, then went into the garage. At the point she realized both her parents were out of the room, she went snooping.

Tanya could hear typing in the den. She peeked through the crack in the door and saw her mother on the computer. A green folder sat next to her, in which she scribbled down notes. Tanya kept as silent as possible.

Her opportunity came when her mother stretched and stood up. Tanya backed out of view, and waited. Then she heard the hallway bathroom door close. She snuck into the den.

The folder contained sheets of notebook paper. A name was listed at the top of each page, with a list of details below:

"Mitch Holden"--wife--Mary, two sons--Daniel & Roger. Police chief. Gets to work at 8:00. Stops at gas station for coffee."

"Tharon Goodbody"--librarian, 73 years old, unmarried, no family. Always brings lunch. Lives on 1430 E 5th Ave."

Each sheet was like this--where they lived, when they went to work, how they got there, what they ate, who were their relatives, age, hobbies, height, weight.

Were they lying to her? Were they stalking people? Good people didn't collect information like this. Were they searching for new victims? Why else would they need to know family members--how many people they'd have to make disappear.

And then she saw a sheet that said "Thomas Pilkington"--reverend at Prince of Peace. Moved to town three months ago. Daughter--Natalie. At the bottom, the words "LIKELY CANDIDATE" were underlined.

Likely candidate? For what? Becoming another vampire? Someone to join their army of the undead?

She left the room, and wondered if there was a page with her name on it.

#

The next day, Natalie handed Tanya a bottle of spring water at the start of class. "Here you go. My dad blessed it. Now it's holy water."

Tanya accepted the bottle. "You didn't tell him what it was for, did you?," she said.

"No, I just said I needed some holy water. He just laughed and blessed my Dasani before school. Now, are you going to do it?"

Tanya regarded the bottle again. "Do I need to use the whole bottle?"

"I don't know. Use as much of it as you can, I guess. If it only works halfway, they're going to know it was you."

"But can't we just report them to the police?"

"Don't you watch the movies? The police never do anything. It's up to you." Natalie took the bottle and shoved it in Tanya's backpack. "They're monsters. They've killed before. You've got to kill them. They're not real humans. You know?"

"Yeah," Tanya said, staring at the floor.

#

Tanya could barely function in school the rest of the day. She kept her eyes trained on the water bottle sticking out of her backpack. Throughout the day, Natalie constantly asked her if she still had it. At the last bell, as she was walking out the door, she pointed at Tanya and said, "Don't forget."

On the way home, Tanya pictured her parents as the monsters she imagined they were. Her mother had fangs dripping with drool and blood. Her father wore a black cloak wrapped around his face, pulling innocent young girls toward him.

By dinner time, she had transferred the bottle's contents to an empty Diet Coke can to be more discreet. She spun it around in her hands under the table, fortified with the knowledge that they needed to be stopped.

"Do you want butter on your peas, Tanya?" her mother chirped.

"No, thank you."

Her mother turned back to the steaming pot. Her father took his place at the table and asked "Did you get any more sleep last night?"

"A little," she said.

Her mom placed their dishes in front of them, already set with peas, meatloaf, and sliced pears. "Here you go."

"Are you still doing okay?" her dad asked.

"Yeah, I'm fine."

"If you have any other questions, we'd be happy to answer them, you know."

"It's all right. It's fine," Tanya said.

Her mom sat down. "Oh, I forgot napkins."

"And knives," her father said, "I'll get it."

Both of them went back into the kitchen. It was as if a divine hand had created the perfect chance for her.

She pulled out the can and poured half the water on her mom's plate and half on her dad's. It disappeared into the gray gravy and pear juice.

The regret struck her immediately--someone was going to die, because of her. But she couldn't turn back now. They were evil, just like the vampires on TV--with capes and blood and fangs.

They came back to the table, all smiles.

"You're not eating?" Victor asked.

"What? Oh," Tanya tore her gaze away from her dad's meatloaf and looked at her own. She picked up her fork and cut away a chunk.

Her father picked up his own fork as her mom distributed napkins. "This smells great," he said. He sliced away a portion in the center. Juice and water spurted from his knife. Tanya stared wide-eyed.

He speared the chunk and raised it to his mouth, a slight smile on his face.

Tanya opened her mouth to say something, but nothing came out.

He put the meatloaf in his mouth and swallowed it in one bite.

"No, don't!" Tanya yelped.

They froze and stared at their daughter.

Tanya burst into tears. "I'm sorry, I'm sorry, I'm sorry," she ranted in her sobs. "I'm so sorry. Natalie told me to. She said you were monsters. I was scared. I was scared, I didn't know. I'm sorry-"

Rose jumped from her seat to comfort her. "Honey, honey, calm down. What are you talking about?" She rubbed Tanya's back. Her father stared bug-eyed and dumbfounded.

Tanya tried to breathe deep. "The holy water... There's holy water... I put holy water in the meatloaf. Natalie gave it to me. She said you were monsters."

"Holy water?" her dad said. He looked at his meatloaf with great interest and fear. "Uhh..."

Rose stared at her husband, as if waiting for something to happen. He shrugged.

"Where did you get the holy water from?" Rose asked.

"From Natalie."

"Natalie who just moved here?" Rose said.

Tanya wiped her eyes. "Yes. I thought you were going to kill her. I saw the green folder and it had a list of names in it.

104

And you had Natalie's father on it. And it said 'likely candidate', and I thought you were going to kill them or make them vampires or something. So she got me the holy water from her father."

"Ohhh..." Her father sat back, relieved.

Rose breathed out. "Reverend Pilkington," she said. "Don't worry, we're not going to do anything to them. That's a list of people who might be potential enemies or hunters."

"When you're a vampire, you keep tabs on new people in town," Victor said.

"Natalie's father is a television evangelist. Do you know what that is?" Rose asked Tanya, who shook her head. "That's someone who runs church like a business. They have big mega-churches with video screens to try and attract people and get a lot of money."

"So then... you're going to be all right?" Tanya asked.

Victor laughed. "Holy water from a faithless preacher is worth less than my spit."

"And you're not going to kill them?"

"No. If they get snoopy, we can move or bribe them or scare them or something. It's happened before."

"You're not upset that I tried to kill you?"

Victor smiled, "People have been trying to kill us for years. Coming from you, it stings a little, but you were confused."

Tanya sobbed again, but this time from joy. She buried her face in her mom's shoulder. "I'm sorry, I'm sorry. I didn't know what to do."

"It's okay, honey," her mom wiped her tears away and tipped her head up.

"I love you, even though you're not my parents. And you're vampires. It's all Natalie's fault."

"You know," Victor said. "You shouldn't let other people influence your thinking, honey. Maybe Natalie's not such a good friend to have."

"What should I do?" Tanya asked. "She said she would tell her parents."

Rose and Victor looked at each other. "Well," her father said. "I might know a way, if you want to hear it."

#

Tanya was looking away, staring out the window, when Natalie walked into class. She threw down her half-shouldered backpack and scooted up to her.

"So?" Natalie said. "Did you do it? Did you get them?"

Tanya continued to stare out the window, as if she didn't hear.

"Hey, Tanya?" Natalie waved her hand. "Did you do it? Did you..." she lowered her voice. "Kill them?"

Tanya rotated her head toward her.

Natalie frowned in confusion. "Well?" she asked.

Tanya slowly shook her head and smiled like a cat with something in her mouth.

"Why not? They're going to kill you, you know. They're going to kill you in the night and drink your blood."

Again, Tanya shook her head left and right.

"Why not?"

Tanya, still smiling, opened her mouth. Two pearl-white fangs dropped from her upper jaw.

"AAAAAAAAAAH!" Natalie screamed. She fell back, trying to escape her desk, but it tumbled with her.

Everyone watched her sprint out of the classroom, except Patty, who saw Tanya spit out the plastic vampire fangs into her palm.

"That was funny," Patty said. "But now she'll really tell her parents."

"That's fine," Tanya said, "I'll just say it was a joke I thought of."

"She might not be your friend anymore."

"A real friend wouldn't make me kill my parents. Vampires or not."

"So then you didn't kill them?"

Tanya shook her head. "They're still my parents, no matter who they are. And like my mom said--blood is thicker than water, but love is thicker than blood."

Tree Fort   Darrell Carmean

This story is not about a specific day or event. This story is about an object—a tree fort. Not an ordinary tree fort, but something that was bigger than all of us.

I can't tell you the exact day, or even year for that matter, our fort was first conceived of. It was around 1974. It was strategically built in a large empty lot behind the church, adjacent to Weideman's truck farm.

Behind the Clyde's home was a massive tree. I'm not a tree person, per se, so I can't tell you what kind it was. It was the kind of massive tree found in small towns—the kind legends were made of. It was so big around that it took 3 kids locking hands to reach around it. The first limbs were 20 feet off the ground. To build a fort in such a tree would have been too large an undertaking, except that we had my brother Kenny in our camp.

My brother Ken was a junior engineer. When it came to tearing things apart and putting them back together, there was no one better. He made counterfeit quarters. He made a go kart out of old pinto parts and a Wisconsin engine that did 60 miles per hour. Most of all, he had dreams. He and Jeff Slabaugh had a design for a submarine they were going to build to explore the pit behind Ester's house. He designed every one of our forts, including this one.

The first thing was to figure a way up the tree. We took railroad spikes and hammered them into the trunk—perfectly spaced. Then came the task of gathering building supplies. We asked all of our dads for lumber and nails—and when that didn't work, we took what we could find like a band of Artful Dodgers.

There were all kinds of places to find stuff and we exhausted them all. We are not talking about some poorly built structure. All of our main support beams were 2 x 6's or 2 x 8's. It was sturdy. It was about 8 feet wide on the first floor.

We decided the tree was big enough for more, and Ken, being the engineer of the group, devised a second floor. It rose another 10 or 15 feet into the tree, smaller but just as sturdy. To get to the second floor, we ascended through a trap door and it provided security from would-be marauders. You never know who might want to take your tree fort. We were prepared.

The second level had drop-down covers over the windows in case of rock or BB gun attacks. We kept a supply of railroad rocks for firing at enemies if needed, *(our favorite rock for throwing by the way)*. We kept a coffee can to pee into, just in case someone was actually daring enough to climb into "our" tree. And yes, we used that line of defense once. We were the rough and tumble Inwood boys, and like most Inwoodians, we didn't take crap from anyone. For my years there, we never lost a battle, we never needed to redesign—and the summer days spent 30 feet off the ground were golden, and have remained so in my memory, and always will. It was a blast.

We did all kinds of things in our tree fort. We were young and crazy, definitely not afraid of heights. We climbed anything we could get a hold of. We held meetings in the tree, planning things to do the next day. Often we found ourselves just sitting, shooting the breeze. It was right next to Weideman's barn. Some of the kids climbed onto the barn roof from the tree. I wonder today what our parents must have thought about our 30 foot palace in the air. Thinking back, it must have been scary for them on some counts—but they let us do it, and knowing what I know now, I love them for that. Back then, we were invincible and our parents let us believe it.

There are probably people who would say the Inwood kids of 1979 were little hellions, destined to never amount to any good. That may be true in some sense, but at the time we had something to be proud of. Yes, we got in trouble once in awhile and maybe we had too much time on our hands, but our tree fort symbolized what was good about Inwood. Resourcefulness, ability, desire and teamwork—just to name a few things that come to mind. When I think about what we accomplished, I am still filled with pride. Not one single parent was involved with the building. All the materials for the tree were hoisted up by the strong hands of rural kids.

We poured our sweat and blood into the work. I remember how it was a "big deal" to us—and how it remains so in my memory. I thoroughly enjoyed growing up in Inwood. I felt sorry for kids that never got the chance to live like we lived. I secretly hope every kid has a "fort" in one form or another. I'll never forget the magic of it all.

Peoria, Il. *
Experimental Form

Joseph Bottomley

Joseph Bottomley and gentle smart Meg stood in the light blue doorway.
Red faces, white hair, gentle smiles.
Come in come in said the spider to the fly.
Pretend a smiling face can be trusted.

Sarah Jane

A brown and white speckled pony in a field of knee high green grass waiting.
Sarah Jane came to ride the pony to the top of the green mountain every day.
One day a little boy of light brown hair came.
He stroked the pony's mane.
Every day. He came.
He rode the small brown and white pony to the top of the green mountain.
He whispered words of encouragement.

Georgina Phelps

A high breasted, wild-eyed, smart ass girl with a tongue sharp as a serpent's tail.
No patience for questions.
Fists tight at her sides, for self control or ready or something.
Furious broads are always looking for a lion tamer.
The kind of guy who will rape you just as soon as say hello.
Living life so hard that it would soften up the tough stringy pulp she called herself.
Plenty of time to wake up, smell the coffee and find the lion tamer before she got herself killed.

Joe parsons

Joe, Joe, what were you thinking signing up for that business, 'your duty'.
Oh mama, Jesus! No place to run, nowhere safe.
Ought to be home where you belong.

Miss Harriet

Miss Harriet was a real lady.
Her sharp hawk nose and creamy skin against henna red hair.
The affection she felt for her chicks in spite of her starch on a medium hanger look.
Kept us wayward girls on the straight and narrow when mom wasn't around.
Her words found a place in the empty caverns called our minds.
Raging hormones playing block and tackle.
When we were through with stupid.
"Sorry it's just me, not Mr. Excitement".
Maybe we might remember.

George and Effie

A nice pair. Good looking. Went together.
She said she never would go to the dreaded mid west to be with her man.
Oh man! More boxes and junk you could fill up a van or two.
Bound together with their brand of loud and clear.
Snarling foes with fangs and claws driven deep to that syrupy spot called love.

Ned and Niles

Walking side by side, an occasional brush of hands, noticeable only to the initiated.
So many secrets, like us.

Georgina Phillips

Stand still truth. Black and white is easy. Not ambiguous grey. The color of life.

Neila Mezynski

Poetry

This Barn

Amy David

forever in limbo,
who will buy indulgences
for its rafters?
Who will listen
as it blames the rope?
Empty since the dusk
it became a grandmother
clock, pendulum swinging
to the door, to the pen
of rabbits, three seconds
in each direction,
long enough for the sky
to pull the blanket
of grass up to its chin
and tuck in for the night,
long enough for my cousin
to split two chickens
from their heads
and pluck them clean
for supper.

When they found her,
nobody noticed
if her fingers had rope burn
I came to ask the dairy cows
if they heard her choke
out cries for help
or only an unwritten note,
if she felt the bruises
appear below her jowls
like a necklace of coal,
if she danced
the Charleston in the air,
if the piss down her leg
kept her toes warm,

if three seconds,
then six,
nine,
twelve,
were long enough for her
to look down
and see the cracking
of eggshells, tiny beaks
poking through.

Dead Wires   Richard Fein

Now the quiet pedestrians are the odd ones.
But just a few years ago,
those who talked to themselves or screamed at phantoms
or literally laughed out loud at their own jokes
were given wide berth on city streets by the silent multitude of passersby.
But change has charged the air with electric oscillations
plugging into ever more breast pockets and pocketbooks.
Loneliness is being shouted down by cell phone cacophony.
The world grows noisier.
Today, the mumbling majority walk the streets in supposed perfect sanity.

So now it's the silent ones who haunt the sidewalks,
the odd wanderers who need no phones,
those to whom no one wants to listen,
those who have no one to listen to,
the disconnected, the never connected,
the brotherhood of the ignored,
the sisterhood of the shunned,
the figurative deaf mutes who travel
beyond all the service areas,
those isolated circuits,
those shaggy frayed dead wires
dangling off the network of the modern world.

My Blackmail Note to All of You   Richard Fein

I bought one for 45 bucks, a plain, planar lens,
but with a tattletale opening on the side of the lens tube,
and inside a privacy-piercing mirror placed at the proper right angle
to reflect all you oblivious peripheral subjects straight into my sharp focus.
Sometimes my camera points at garbage cans for it isn't beauty I seek,
but your faux pas beauts committed when you think no one is looking.
With my make-believe-forward-facing lens all your venial embarrassments center in my vision.
I'm the candid camera of public parks unabashedly pointing my peeping Tom lens at all of you—
nose pickers, crotch scratchers, earwax scoopers, bellybutton lint pickers, navel ponderers,
bra adjusters, food dribblers, sweaty underarm raisers, and egregious expectorating phlegm throwers.
I also frame what holy zealots regard as mortal sins,
lovers unzipping flies—girl and boy of course,
but also male and male for a double uncoupling of zippered teeth.
And even clearer naked truths are uncovered by my tabloid lens,
bearded Moslems eyeing Orthodox Jewish girls draped in long denim skirts,
and Chassids eyeing every blond shiksa passing by.
(Mortal sin or not, maybe, just maybe hush-hush hankering might someday bring Holy Land peace.)
A menagerie of piggish improprieties of the purportedly priggish
played out at the perimeter of my perception all fall perpendicular
to my presumed but pseudoline of sight and are then pivoted
precisely to my picture-taking peepers.
Listen, I've got all your gotcha moments ensconced on my memory card,
perturbing pixels primed for planetary propagation via a grand upload to the worldwide web.

Of course extortion is prohibited, but it's permissible,
constitutionally protected to photograph
people's private peccadillos performed in public places,
and I'm not asking for even a penny from anyone.
No, I'm asking for so much more from everyone.

Possible Parallel Other   Richard Fein

Basic principle of Locality: The Physicist's commonsense notion about events,
that there's a distance and time passed between a cause and its effect
Electron pair: two electrons that occupy the same orbital but have opposite spins.

After the Big Bang came the primal diaspora,
the great wandering of everything across the Sinai of absolute nothing.
Maybe, just maybe, electron pairs sharing opposite spins were pulled apart,
separated soon after the birth of all being,
yet still possessing an interstellar hankering for each other,
an immutable desire to dance a do-si-do of spins.
For the laws of quantum physics
make us all uncertainties, flickering clouds of possibilities.
And sibling electrons must always twirl in opposite directions
so if one reverses spin then the other must also immediately
no matter how far apart and in disobedience to Locality.
And for this paradox the physicists can describe merely what happens but not why.
Why, a question only a sentient creature could answer or dare to ask.
Thus within me some particular electron turns now one way but perhaps someday in reverse,
while somewhere beyond Ursa Major, Orion, or Crab Nebula it has a possible lost sibling
within some other sentient being who also scans the sky asking why.
I and my possible parallel other, infinitely far apart but forever linked,
two sentient souls, two mere containers for two electrons twirling in tandem dance.

A Glutton for Truth   Richard Fein

The proof is in the pudding,
but what exactly does that mean?
80%, 90%, 100% proof, I'd drink to that,
then flop face down into the mushy mess.
And what kind of pudding holds such dispositive evidence,
plum? vanilla? chocolate? bread?
or perhaps tropical tapioca after the cyanide is boiled off?
The old saw is a mangled adage.
The actual sixteenth century proverb is—
the proof of the pudding is in the eating.
Ergo,
the proof is in the pudding
is not exactly the truth, the whole truth, and nothing but.
And to eat the pudding is to eat the proof.
In short, you can't have your proof and eat it too.
Besides, a bellyful of truth will bloat your stomach,
and who wants to be near such a gasbag.
What to do with truth and its pudding proof.
You can sniff around it
or observe its quivering nature,
but if you open your big mouth and swallow
then you deny it to others just as hungry for it,
and who also believe they
really want to taste the slimy concoction.
Swallow truth and truth is within you,
and thereafter you must be the mold
and not the pudding that the mold shapes.

This Statement Is False,   Richard Fein

if it's false then it's true, if it's true then it's false,
a well-worn ancient Greek philosopher's paradox.
But our world is neither true nor false, it's a universe of maybes
or worse
a cosmos of truths proven false.
"This statement is false" vouches for its own veracity,
a dizzying self-reference like a dog chasing its own tail,
a declarative sentence that either stands or falls but can't lean
somewhere in between.
The sentence subject—statement—doesn't stand outside the
statement it's in
and therein lies the paradox.
Another ancient Greek philosopher, Protagoras, coined yet
another old Hellenic saw,
"Man is the measure of all things . . . ."
Yes Man in this sentence is the subject but a subject that doesn't
self-reference itself,
the dog chases not its own tail but the cat's.
But in this aphorism Man embodies all women and men,
and each one takes one's own measure for that is what makes one
human
and not a mere beehive drone or sterile female worker in that
crowded nest.
Thus all measures are the measure of all things,
but when all things are measured by all measures nothing is
measured.
Therein lies yet another putative paradox, "Nothing is the
measure of all things."
Protagoras was an agnostic and lived not by the certainty of true
or false,
but was for a lifetime haunted by the almighty maybe.
But consider "God is the measure of all things," then if there's
only one God
with no subset divinities— behold no paradox.
"God is the measure of all things," a sophism of monotheistic
belief,
a simple declarative sentence that is either true or false
but truly forms no syntax of false maybes.

A Guilt-Free Sorry — Richard Fein

"Dear applicant, we're sorry to say no to you."
But if no brings sorrow why say it?
Wouldn't a yes salve your sadness?
Sorry? the word's lack of nuance nags me,
for it's such a guilt-free sorry.
Your rejection of my application didn't use words like
repent, atone, contrite or remorse
for such words imply a sorry of your own doing,
a sorry that screams for undoing.
But there's no hope of that, is there?
No hope of you including me among you.
You hand me just a perfunctory sorry
and of course an insincere sincerely yours.
You probably forgot about me the moment you mailed that sorry
to "applicant's address."
Or maybe you're still having a condescending laugh over my application,
and your sorry is really a euphemistic snicker.
But sorry to me is real.
Repent, atone, contrite, are also real,
and I use them now remorselessly.
I repent, atone, and am very contrite
that I applied to you in the first place.
And so I also declare with my deepest guilt-free sorry,
that you have not deigned to elect into your grand collegiums—
me, myself, and I, the one most skilled in crafting the sincerest
sorriest of we're sorry
to all those pretentious enough to apply for inclusion among your
minions.

Annual Autumn Exodus

Derek Richards

cheers are ripe
at the old football stadium
sticky green leaves
shed weight, wither, color,
fall

is the nickname for autumn
my liquored up folly of friends
we must begin the detox rituals,
the rehab application processes,
winter is coming
soon

and new england winters
are no blessing for the homeless
we might even walk
to florida
if we had new shoes

let us leave this park
march crowded down the boulevard
i will be moses
i know a shortcut

Directions on how to ruin a town: Derek Richards
How god spoke through Bradley

dacatia was a passive village
mountain-snug and rarely stumbled upon

except for a few rollerskaters
searching steep hills for death

and i lived there, making my living
lining coffins with red velvet

looking forward to the isolation of winter
hot apple cider and roasted chicken

but you, my god, tore through as scissors
named bradley with greetings from bel air

after just a month the town newspaper
listed twelve accounts of a miracle

and the editor began to privately worry
that *The Dacatia View* would slip into tabloid

then came that date, october 22, a sunday
when you spoke through bradley to a crowd

of merchants and skiers at the local hotel
claiming the town's water would stifle aging

allowing the beneficiary a lifetime of hammocks
and august lemonade and maybe even sex

but only if combined with *Bel Air Salsa*
as a vicious drink of the lord

bradley told of god testing the concoction
on a five year old dog named missy

who was born during the great depression
when my little town was just a well

Fort Gloucester
Derek Richards

jagged granite slabs apparently
drip
and slant

arousing a hurries series
of splash
and spray

and because i am borrowing another name
walking in waist-less shorts
sadly drunk on the wine
of used stories

the role of your hair will be played
by the breeze
the silk voice offered to shadows
the fate of this fort
romantic and degraded and simply

i am homeless
often persuaded to forgive kindness
suffer sympathy
and remind tourists
you've been known to linger

as some century smoldering
slip
and fade

allowing the teeth of this ocean
a bruise to bite
and sink

With Apologies to the Girl behind the Counter

seven minutes after my car crash
with a lawyer and his attorney,
I arrive bruised and severely stoned
on shock. the idea of waiting in a line
transforms my best smile
into a grin with bite.

a man six people ahead of me talks
to his cell phone,
*she's got about as much chance
as Indiana winning the Big Ten in football, ya know?*
the rest of us squirm in front
of an array of such items of interest
as a 5 Hour Energy bar and walnut-raisin cookies.

*no, you're right. maybe i'll tell her.
okay. we're still on for sunday, right?*
he laughs. *i got twenty on Dallas
and i don't lose, remember?*

suddenly the woman in front of me
clears her throat,
*are we examining each purchase today
or could we just ring the fucking things up?*
i nod my head and look
at the girl behind the counter.
red hair, pale skin, a galaxy
of cinnamon freckles across her cheeks and arms.

she pretends not to hear the comments,
focusing instead on the debit card
currently in her hands..
that'll be twenty-two fifty-seven, she says.
slide-punch-sign.
now i'm four people away from escape.

and then it hits me,
sudden and disfiguring as a stroke:

i have no empathy. none.
all the muscles in my shoulders and back
tense because she is not perfect,
she is not blinding fast at her job,
and despite her nice features,
she's not attractive
enough to distract me from my frustrations.

how are you today, sir?
nodding my head, i slide my purchase
across the counter and reach for my wallet.
i'm fine. just fine. how are you?
i'm fine. just fine. thank you.

seconds before i'm about to escape,
i hear a scratchy baritone clear his throat.
this girl on meds or something?
i stare into her eyes and see nothing.
here's your receipt.
thank you. have a nice day.
you too.

the exit doors buzz open
and the sunshine stings, instant and pure.
i've got to call my lawyer later
about the car crash with the lawyer,
but for now, i think about nothing
except cinnamon freckles,
cold eyes unblinking behind a counter.

Derek Richards

Riddance to Riddles   Derek Richards

what happens when you throw a yellow rock
into a purple stream?
i don't know.
so i asked old billy knowles,
the moonshine genius of nugent farms.

*a burst of raw grapefruit spits around your head like cocaine fingers
on a spinning wheel*

before my brain exploded
i said goodbye to old billy knowles,
caught the high-noon train to lake shore
where aunt middy-may can be found
writing sonnets in dog blood.

what happens when you throw a yellow rock
into a purple stream?

*christ our gentle lord removes the stain of three-chord blues
from our humble lives*

leaving lake shore i decided
the answer could be downtown
at jakes jelly saloon.
growing out of the maple bar,
low-tide larry,
vodka priest of the local clam flats.

what happens when you throw a yellow rock
into a purple stream?

*ain't about the colors, son. it's about the splash. my advice, stop eating
crayons*

Common Sounds   George Moore

The world rubs up against itself here,
on the rolling hills of the out-of-the-way,
and yet the horses are belled, and every
bow of the head brings in a chorus full
of discordant 21st-century sounds,
wrapped in the old iron clang of history.

The cattle are no better. They never stand
complete still, and their cowbells go off
at all hours of the night, and they low against
the loss of one, of any that wander off.

The sheep too are collared with thin iron
sounds, the shepherds are saying this
is the way it has always been, each lamb
knows the sound of its mother's bell,
each shepherd knows its flock's movement
by the cymbal thin peels of distant sound

that rises up across the sparse oak fields,
flowing like a wave through heavy air,
a ring that becomes a symphony of chimes
anonymous as rain beating on the roof.

The Santa Fe Trail

George Moore

The galleries have opened like jaws
to welcome the scurrying and terrified
tourists of the June day, who would
leave the sun-blindness outside, the dry air,

to enter the beautiful, the painterly,
the pure of their own indigenous link.
But then it rains. Along the road
are blown out tires and scrapes of tread

that lead to the last casino, a trail
of the dead leading the dead, and then
the soon-to-be, who have not yet spent
their children's inheritance.

The pottery here is unique, made
of the raw earth, black and red,
and going for more than a miner makes
in a lifetime of bucketing up the dirt.

The writers come, to capture in words
the light as the painters have seen it,
illuminating the rose hills to the west,
near the nuclear facilities at Los Alamos.

From L.A. come the rest, the hordes
of humanity, the escapees from a coastal
malaise, from the worn-out, smoke-
choked freeways to hell, having cross

too often for a quickie weekend
in Tijuana, and now looking for heaven,
or anything else. And they find rest,
behind the adobe walls now

made of concrete, and rise late
in the evening to enjoy the simmering
tableside service, that cooks the veal
under just the right heat.

The Place

George Moore

The place where I was raised does not exist
anymore, or it has changed through rough weather,
through earthquakes and violent sandstorms,

to be what it always was, another place, the Other
of landscapes, changed from the day I left.
There are still trees that pretend to know the difference

and the creek still dribbles through the backyards,
but the people there are from another planet,
another time, they have faces without expressions,

unlike those I remember when I was young,
the faces, each one, that would salute me openly
as a child. Now this place is full of adults,

and I am the worst one. Now that secret warmth
of the day, the grass grown just a little too long,
the sleepy avenue that no one ever drove,

now it's only the memory of another place
where nothing ever went wrong, nothing was ever
out of place, the days were secretly the same.

The world grew no more than a few feet tall,
and ended at the forest edge, where there was a trail
that everyone said went no place.

One Night Stay

Howie Good

An old man with eyes like dead sparrows
is telling a story at the next table
in the restaurant of the Quality Inn
in Lebanon, Pennsylvania, something
about the price of scrap metal after the war.
Suddenly he lowers his voice. The Jews,
he mumbles. My wife and I look at each other.
Meat hooks. Gas chambers.
Our daughter notices. What? she asks.
I shake my head. We finish eating
and go up to our $74-a-night room
and all lie on one bed and watch TV.
The studio audience is laughing.

Inwood Park   By johnmac the bard

The top of Manhattan Island
-- not, though, the top of
the borough of Manhattan
(but that's another story)
where the Indians fleeced
Peter Minuit.

Fields for baseball, football,
and Irish sports
Courts for basketball, tennis,
handball, and horseshoes
(we called those "pits").

and, the "woods" – a forest with
paths, caves, and hidden places
where we learned to smoke
(implanting cancer cells into
many of our lungs) and
drink (beginning the deterioration of
brain and liver cells for many).

and couples often moved from the
benches in the park to the woods
for more privacy .. but, in those days,
there was no fucking (or, at least,
none that I knew about).

We would have been better
off fucking (if we had known
about safe sex) – some of us
who weren't fucking later
died of lung cancer or cirrhosis.

It's still a wonderful park

The Bars

by johnmac the bard

I grew up in an Irish/Jewish neighborhood
the Jewish lads went to school and studied
the Irish went to the bars.

To be sure, many of us also went to school
and played sports and went out with girls
(no sex, though)
but we went to the bars
underage
after games
after dates
after softball games
before and after dances
to watch the Sunday football game
and for every other damn reason.

the Broadstone
the Wiilow Tree, Erin's Isle
Chambers', McSherry's, the Inwood Longue
Doc Fiddler's, Cassidy's, Jimmy Ryan's, Keenan's Corner
Dolan's, The Pig n' Whistle, Freehill's, Terminal, Old Shiling
Markey's. McGolderick's, Carmor, Roonry's, Grippo's, Minogue's
well, you get the idea

We knew the bartenders by name
George Lynch, Pat Gallagher, "Sunshine", Georgie Costello,
Chris, Fred, Tommy, Mara, Dan, John, Joe, Kathy-in-Erin's
and they all bought back "The next one's on me, Mac"
(and you never leave after a buyback)

We hung out there
we talked
we laughed
we sang
we sometimes fought
.. and we drank

But we didn't just drink in the bars
we drank in the park
we drank at parties
we drank at football games
we drank at dances (from a hidden flask)

Many slowed down as the grew up
many stopped altogether
and some were stopped only by the grave.

"The drink" was a macho factor
If you told a fellow he had diabetes,
he'd stop taking sugar.
If you told some of my friends that
they shouldn't drink, they'd say
"What do you mean? I can hold my liquor"

They planned to drink until they died
and they did.

I still think we had more fun
than the Jewish guys
(unless they were getting laid)

The Friday Night Dance　　　by johnmac the bard

On Friday night, we'd get
suited up and head down to
our local Catholic Grammar School
for a teen age dance
(when we got a bit older,
we'd kill a ½ pint of
Old Mr. Boston Lemon
Flavored Vodka first)

I'd be wrapped around a girl
in a slow dance, my hand caressing
he hair as my torso tried to join hers
when Father Devine would wander
over and say
"Leave room for the Holy Ghost"

That statement might gave opened up
space between some other bodies
but I would make the point that
"the Holy Ghost is spiritual, Father;
he can fit anywhere he wants"
(fifty years later, after winning a Silver
Star as a Vietnam chaplain, he still
remembers those remarks)

If a young lady returned after such a dance
to dance again, she had to really like me
for I would have been singing in her ear
with the worst singing voice in the world.

Oh, well; it was prior to the pill and
these girls didn't put out anyhow.
… so we drank.

1958   by johnmac the bard

I drive deep into the right corner and go up in the air,
hang for an instant, and get nothing but net!
Afterwards, one of the players on our younger team,
Vinnie Berndetto asks me how I stay up in the air so long.
Vinnie died last week.

I clear a rebound, turn, and hit Buddy Kelly streaking
downcourt for a layup
Buddy died over 10 years ago.

Bob Cummings takes a rebound, gives to me and
I find John Marai with a bounce pass as he cuts
to the basket – two more points!
Both Bob and John are dead for over ten years.

After the game, coach Jim McArdle pats me on the
ass and says "Nice game"
Jim's been dead for over twenty years.

Bob Gorman and Jerry Moran walk up the stairs with
me to the locker room.
They're both gone too.
Sometimes I remember too much.

The Journey to Me — Lynda Nash

'The city nothing but rooftops!' you'd say
So we'd walk to the country,
collect litter from the hillside,
laughing like flower children.

You believed in anarchy. I did too.
We picked daffodils in public places.
Sat up all night talking of aesthetics, music, life.

You said, 'all property is theft.
Employment's for idlers.'
I helped fund your appeals,
understood when you needed
a little something to help you sleep.

Before long you could not see
beauty without substance.
We'd rush to the country
but see nothing but hedge tops
and a pit-stop for refreshment
before the dark jaunt home.

Our concurrent lives unsynchronized.
When the police called regarding
a naked man at the window,
I concealed the mescaline
on the mantelpiece.

The night you saw
God behind a cushion
   signified the end.

Vitamin injections were painful.
So we'd walk the grounds
to find a secluded spot
for your self indulgence.

Doctors asked why I stayed.
They weren't to know
I'd never been alone.
That I was a stranger,
to everyone but you.

In Transit   Lynda Nash

I met a man who wrote poetry on buses.
Not in magic marker on seat backs
or spray-paint on ceilings.
In a dog-eared notebook he inscribed letters so tiny
the bobbing heads could not eavesdrop on his journey.
Once, he said, he'd travelled all the way
to Paris, France, without looking up.
He planned to travel to Paris, Texas one day
but feared America too vast a country for such a small pen.
If the ink ran out how would he find his way home?

On His Own Path — Lynda Nash

'I'm a poet,' he announced, one morning at the bus station.
The words filtered through benches, became a distant echo
but, like the newspaper dancing against the Perspex,
no one gave him a transient glance or cursory nod.

'I'm a poet,' he told himself every afternoon in the shop window.
A positive affirmation, for confirmation
in case life may have altered course over night.

He grew a beard, stopped combing his hair,
wandered the streets in search of meaningful things
to write on the back of cigarette packets or polystyrene cartons.

He listened for colour in language –
nothing inspiring about urban-speak or the chatter of clerks
as they scurried like ants from platform to office.
Rappers without rhythm,
loose change singing a mantra in their pockets.

'I'm a poet!' he shouted, to the girls glowing under the streetlight,
while the city fell from pubs and clubs and toppled into tube
stations,
the spoils of their day spilling into gutter as he delved.

'I'm a poet,' he sighed. 'I should live in the country,
have affinity with nature, experience the rawness of life.'
Then shook his fist and cursed the city
for its lack of trees and birds and limitless sky.

'I'll be leaving now,' he whispered to the pavement,
folded his cardboard bed and followed his own path to
inspiration.

Unexpected Guests — Lynda Nash

Please do not leave when I scream.
I am not a child, easily frightened
By the white outlined shape of a man,
leaning over my husband as he sleeps,
until my cry awakes him to see no-one.
It was just a surprise to discover
another person in the room.

Please do not leave when I scream.
I am an adult, old enough not to be afraid,
as you stand around my headboard
while my husband works night shift.
I only left the room check the children.

Having made the effort to visit
why not stay a little longer?
I'd like to converse (if possible)
to look at your clothes,
see what you hold in your hands.
I ran out to fetch a friend
So they could meet you too.

Ignore my pounding heartbeat,
waking up to find your face staring into mine
was quite a shock!
You need not have disappeared.

If you return, I will promise not to scream.
If you promise not to leave when I do.

St. Deroin
Mary Marie Dixon
(Nebraska ghost town)

The moon inflames all darkened streets,
Her liquored haze a whitened waste
Where raccoons bandit for gluttonies
And wash their catch of ill-gotten gains.

Cathedral spires of cottonwoods cast scorn
On wanton mice who ravage groceries
Of grain in irrigated streets of corn;
An owlish vengeance thwarts reprieve.

The coyote's heated howl cajoles
To gain. He is a starry heaving profiteer.
All shadows, miles away from parish souls,
Cover the glare unleashed by godly fear.

The cockled burr infenced by scrutiny
Laments the neighborly obscurity.

Spirits of Chickens
Mary Marie Dixon

My mother wrung the necks of chickens
in the back yard, and we
brought boiling water
for their dismembered bodies.

The shaft feathers so deep,
they had to be plucked one by one.
A sifting down on undersides
to save for feather pillows.

The yellow feet are useless claws,
scaley handled stems
on white orchids, disrobed to pink
and tender veining.

The chestnut tree dropped
its ripened Buckeyes,
glazed over brown,
in the passing season.

Death, not much blood,
a delicate spray of red.
A flour sack, a cast iron pan,
Speckled brown bits.

Rolling lard browned the roux;
My mother stirred cream gravy.
We set the table and spread lace
under the centerpiece.

We say the meal-time prayer.
Not much thought
to the simple grace.
We pass the relish tray.

Radish bulbs and onion stalks;
the spirits of chickens alive
inside the hands
that have taken their heads.

House

Mary Marie Dixon

your
       body

     twisted in '27
by the tornado
    that provoked
Grandpa to dig
        the root cellar

    my mother said
there wasn't a square corner in you

washed white
     you bloomed
          up over prairie dust
    may day '34

you were
    ration for
Grandma's second son
       whose hunting
    produced no wild meat
           in that '45 Italian transport

   '64
   on your linoleum lap
   my 2 sisters and 4 brothers
played in split lines where chairs rubbed

 an inherited acreage '74
 your
     frame
     expanded even as
        it spilled
           two

your

```
        face
        from the inside out
                shone at night
                        in the dark country nights
  coming home '85



now

your
        skin
                disturbed plaster
        over slat bones

your
        dressing gown
                wallpaper
                        flowers peeled to olive
                then mauve rouge

your
        shoulders
                        tiered up
                under sagging eaves

you see
        with crackled eyes
                and smoke panes

'04 out of your
        reach
                a tapered
                        plume
        down burns
                your twisted
                        body
```

Gingerbread Lady

Michael Lee Johnson

Gingerbread lady,
no sugar or cinnamon spice;
years ago arthritis and senility took their toll.
Crippled mind moves in then out, like an old sexual adventure
blurred in an imagination of fingertip thoughts.
Who remembers the characters?
There was George, her lover, near the bridge at the Chicago River:
she missed his funeral; her friends were there.
She always made feather-light of people dwelling on death,
but black and white she remembers well.
The past is the present; the present is forgotten.
Who remembers Gingerbread Lady?
Sometimes lazy-time tea with a twist of lime,
sometimes drunken-time screwdriver twist with clarity.
She walks in scandals; sometimes she walks in soft night shoes.
Her live-in maid smirked as Gingerbread Lady gummed her food,
false teeth forgotten in a custom-imprinted cup
with water, vinegar, and ginger.
The maid died. Gingerbread Lady looks for a new maid.
Years ago, arthritis and senility took their toll.
Yesterday, a new maid walked into the nursing home.
Ginger forgot to rise out of bed;
no sugar, or cinnamon toast.

Harvest Time

Michael Lee Johnson

A Métis Indian lady, drunk,
hands blanketed as in prayer,
over a large brown fruit basket
naked of fruit, no vine, no vineyard
inside-approaches the Edmonton,
Alberta adoption agency.
There are only spirit gods
inside her empty purse.
Inside, an infant,
restrained from life,
with a fruity wine sap apple
wedged like a teaspoon
of autumn sun
inside its mouth.
A shallow pool of tears
mounts in native blue eyes.
Snuffling, the mother offers
a slim smile, turns away.
She slithers voyeuristically
through near slum streets,
and alleyways,
looking for drinking buddies
to share a hefty pint
of applejack wine.

Charley Plays a Tune

Michael Lee Johnson

Crippled, in Chicago,
with arthritis
and Alzheimer's,
in a dark rented room,
Charley plays
melancholic melodies
on a dust filled
harmonica he
found abandoned
on a playground of sand
years ago by a handful of children
playing on monkey bars.
He now goes to the bathroom on occasion,
relieving himself takes forever; he feeds the cat when
he doesn't forget where the food is stashed at.
He hears bedlam when he buys fish at the local market
and the skeleton bones of the fish show through.
He lies on his back riddled with pain,
pine cones fill his pillows and mattress;
praying to Jesus and rubbing his rosary beads
Charley blows tunes out his
celestial instrument
notes float through the open window
touch the nose of summer clouds.
Charley overtakes himself with grief
and is ecstatically alone.
Charley plays a solo tune.

Nikki Purrs

Michael Lee Johnson

Soft nursing
5 solid minutes
of purr
paws paddling
like a kayak competitor
against ripples of my
60 year old river rib cage-
I feel like a nursing mother
but I'm male and I have no nipples.
Sometimes I feel afloat.
Nikki is a little black skunk,
kitten, suckles me for milk,
or affection?
But she is 8 years old a cat.
I'm her substitute mother,
afloat in a flower bed of love,
and I give back affection
freely unlike a money exchange.
Done, I go to the kitchen, get out
Fancy Feast, gourmet salmon, shrimp,
a new work day begins.

Rod Stroked Survival with a Deadly Hammer   Michael Lee Johnson

Rebecca fantasized that life was a lottery ticket or a pull of a lever,
that one of the bunch in her pocket was a winner or the slots
were a redeemer;
but life itself was not real that was strictly for the mentally insane
at the Elgin
Mental Institution.
She gambled her savings away on a riverboat
stuck in mud on a riverbank, the Grand Victoria, in Elgin,
Illinois.
Her bare feet were always propped up on wooden chair;
a cigarette dropped from her lips like morning fog.
She always dreamed of traveling, not nightmares.
But she couldn't overcome, overcome,
the terrorist ordeal of the German siege of Leningrad.
She was a foreigner now; she is a foreigner for good.
Her first husband died after spending a lifetime in prison
with stinging nettles in his toes and feet; the second
husband died of hunger when there were no more rats
to feed on, after many fights in prison for the last remains.
What does a poet know of suffering?
Rebecca has rod stroked survival with a deadly mallet.
She gambles nickels, dimes, quarters, tokens tossed away,
living a penniless life for grandchildren who hardly know her
name.
Rebecca fantasized that life was a lottery ticket or the pull of a
lever.

Mother, Edith, at 98
Michael Lee Johnson

Edith, in this nursing home
blinded with macular degeneration,
I come to you with your blurry
eyes, crystal sharp mind,
your countenance of grace-
as yesterday's winds
I have chosen to consume you
and take you away.
"Oh, where did Jesus disappear
to", she murmured,
over and over again,
in a low voice
dripping words
like a leaking faucet:
"Oh, there He is my
Angel of the coming."

The Big Event

Mike Berger

In a little town there isn't much
to do. You would attend all the high
school football games. You do so
even when it's a losing season.
Promptly at 10 o'clock they roll up
the sidewalks. The place becomes
a ghost town except the kids are up.
They park on the hill above the town
just for something to do.

There is one exception to this placid
place. Town folks look forward to
it like a kid looks forward to Christmas.
It's when the only store in town holds
its annual sock sale.

The sale is the chance for the townsfolk
to strip off the thin veneer of civility.
The sale lasts for four hours and it's
catch as catch can. Two hundred
people jammed in the 40 x 40 room,
bashing and thrashing each other over
pairs of socks.

I suppose, the sox are just an excuse
to let down their hair. You have bragging
rights when you've been bashed by an old
ladie's purse. The frenzy lasts until
noon. You grab and armload of socks
and tuck it tightly under your arm. With
the other arm you fight off the would be
sock bandits. You really haven't arrived
until you've spilt a little blood.

When at last the clock strikes twelve,
the sox all go off sale and there is no
excuse to bludgeon your neighbor.
Everyone smiles and are friends again
until they do it again next year.

A Dream Come True

Mike Berger

It was cherry. No dings or dents.
No rust spots. It rested on cinder
blocks. The tires still had air. The
upholstery was worn but clean.
Better yet, no oil spots. Beneath
the dust the paint was still bright.

I dreamed of owning one when I
was in my twenties. With school
and a wife it wasn't to be. Still I
hungered to get behind the wheel
and lay a patch.

At last I have the chance to fulfill my
youthful dream. I dickered hard for that
sixty-seven Mustang. And now it's mine.
I shook and trembled as I took my
first drive. It wasn't the excitement.
You shake a little when you're
seventy-nine.

The Apotheosis of Ugly — Mike Berger

When I speak of a model, most men
think of a beautiful woman.

But my model is a hag from the streets.
We talked as I sketched. I said that
she must have had an interesting life.

She smiled a contorted grin, missing
two front teeth. She corrected me saying
that life wasn't interesting, it was more
like hell.

I asked about the deep scar on her cheek.
"It came from a jealous boyfriend," she
answered. Opening her mouth and
pointed to the hole where teeth should be
"Same guy, still I love him," she said.

It all started when she was fifteen. She
was gang raped behind the high school
bleachers. She was too embarrassed and
afraid to tell anyone.

Each line on her face marked a drunken stupor
where she tried to drown her pain. Her left
shoulder was droopy, arthritic from sleeping on
the ground

Her face was gray; she had matted brown hair that clung to her dirty face. She was more than happy with the 20 bucks I paid her for posing. She said that for $20 she would dance on the table or most anything else.

When we were finished, she wanted to see my work. She stared deeply into the canvas. Tears welled up in her eyes and splashed down her cheeks. She choked out, "Do I really look like that?"

Progress   Mike Berger

The tired old chalky brick
was no match for the massive
steel blade. The scruffy man at
the controls plowed with precision.

Section by section succumbed;
tumbling over it in chunks. The
roar of the diesel engine grew
as the blade shoot into foundation.

Toppled domino tracks scarred
the earth. The beep beep beep
of those are in reverse announced
another pass.

The quaint old Victorian home
stood in the way of progress. Its
demise was quick; no witnesses,
funeral or eulogies.

A twisted mass of rubble would make
way for modern convenience. It would
be replaced by a cold gray concrete
parking terrace.

"On a Magpie"　　　　　　　　Phillip A. Ellis

A handsome magpie,
resplendent, handsome magpie,
strode in the rain. Drops
sleekly slid along his dress
and onto the grass
thirsting for more, then he stopped.
Out puffed his feathers.
In a second, sleek hauteur
turned to wet, weary
resignation. Not one note
sang he, this magpie.
Over the months, and seasons,
magpie feathers fell
until in white and sable
stood sweet sir magpie,
sleek, sweet resplendent magpie,
weary, waterlogged magpie.

"No Regrets" Phillip A. Ellis

In eighty-nine years,
I've forgotten too much
important stuff, except
how to make daisy chains.
My sister taught me.

"On a News Report" — Phillip A. Ellis

She says, "Oh. How
terrible. How could a man
do that to his kids."
It's such a terrible waste."
Some time earlier
today, he'd picked up his kids
for it's Saturday.
And by the time cicadas
and the sun combined
to exorcise the shadows,
and the sky's that weight,
the kids were asleep. Curled tight
like the skies and light,
their lips remained blue. And in
her chair, my mother
says how terrible it is
for all mothers. That
it's such a waste, a mother
would never do that,
vainly so as to forget
those that have.

"After Night-Rain" Phillip A. Ellis

At some point, I'll wake
and it will be dark outside.
There'll be a frog, out
there somewhere, and with its call
I'll remember years
in a city still between
mountains and ocean.
There it was I knew the song
of wind taking trees
five hours walk away, across
orange streetlights. there
detonators just after
midnight. No more now
can I feel again that way,
without remembering them.

"A Memory of the Old Farm"   Phillip A. Ellis

I remember the parting after.
We were beneath the ancient
apple trees, by the outhouse
inhabited by accretions of refuse
from the fallen farmhouse.
We shared, as it were, an absinthe,
seeing in each a newly awakened
adult in one, and a slowly dying
dream in the other. It is pleasant
to awake in the afternoon beneath
the gum trees, and to know
for the moment of awakening,
the cicadas are resting in the sleek blue
of a deepening sky. With that parting,
and the falling away of childhood,
so too fell the last of untrammeled summers,
and a twice-long storm.

Local Enterprise

    How many wrecks   can you sell   from the driveway
or the front yard   -- before   the neighbors
   tell you quit   -- how many sportsthings or sedans --
decently   patched   and   sprayed --
   how many credit aps scratch out   -- for kids let down
by whispering   -- thinking   themselves
   some throb   -- and   no harm   satisfied   -- as if
it were stones alone   that   played   their tricks
   on   cornering? A weekend   in   Time's   made up
in plastic stars   and   touring wheels
   / a weekend in minds made up   -- designing complaints
against the stacks   / against   this red   men swear
   they've never seen the likes of   -- and ten dollar suits --
crisp pressed   -- to the far side of fashionable.
   You're glad for the chill some nights   -- glad for the green
and seventy   -- for the looks of kids   -- renewed
   in an old contest   -- because it's the weekend after all --
arranged in the skirts   and   deafening comics
   and tiered lighting   -- these cameras   about   as busy
as the close stars get. By then   they'll   have
   sensed   the jugular   -- forgetting   the driveway spills --
the bondo   / bakes   and   cross-styled   harmonics --
   the credit risks   -- signing   their lives   on anything --
as if a machine   -- restored   -- might redesign
   the universe   -- as if a whim so / a strategy so cauterized
relaxed the heart to industry   / the will to miscreate --
   and   was   and   is   -- obsessing the speed-minded
and   phrase-starved   -- a   silhouette
   yard-company   -- decided the meats   they'll serve up
Sundays at the brink   -- gossiping   skirts
   and quoting   half-time comics   sneaking sips. Hadn't
the sales   / skids   / the soaped lines --
   spelling prices out   -- and the dump crews   -- cursing
the farm pups   / the ends of wild things   -- hosing
   what's left   to   the brief green green   and afterwards --
the music   been good enough   for you   -- hearing
   the scoped joints   roaring   through   some lifetimes --
draped   in   these   steam-pressed   threads --

fit enough for smiling?   Except   for the mirrored floors
and   post-football heroics   -- what's   there to say
   for all of it   -- except   for the tiered lights   -- winking
away or out   -- what's   to be said   for fall --
   for the desires   / ranks   -- for   this rain   blown off --
over the stadium seats   and   novelty post-boxes --
   over the graves   on the hill routes   -- into   the sheds
drawn down   by   seasons   as they passed   -- into
   the face of jack   -- springing to light in an old costume --
about as funny as this gets   -- given   the costs
      and   over-runs   / the tracks   and   product spirals
/ the leaves   -- as   they rain   off mullberries --
   littering the tracked sponge lawn   -- tracks left by wrecks
you'd turned on an initial   -- by the wrecks
   no one   in his worst dreams   was purchasing. Hadn't
you thought straight out   -- and one more way
   of making it? But   nothing surprises   anymore. And
you   -- in no flat way confederate   -- imagine
      the dreams chased west   -- to the high plains or Indiana --
the boxes of dreams men leave   -- windows broken in --
wide to the moonlight's now   -- or anybody's salvage.
Why   wouldn't   the moving lights   / the
   tresseled lights   / the cold   explain   this company --
the sagas they sprayed on stone   / the curses
      they   sprayed   against   the state   -- against
the corporate planners   -- sporting
      their   corporate   meals   underbelt   -- and
nothing   themselves   maybe   -- in
      no   flat way   confederate   -- mistaking
for   their   own
      old songs   the planners   never
         had the hearts for?

Robert Lietz

Learning To Speak Her Own Name Twice

    Any other room or any other solitaire!
She oils the teak and lets that sit.
    The parts she had thought they'd stock
have kept her waiting days --
    watching the trucks perform   / the days
add up in terrible fists and grid-irons --
    boys with their blames to bear   -- and
voluble schoolings   -- feeling
    fall   come on   -- in   the bean-rows
and   the rock-maples. She   oils
    the teak   and   lets that sit   -- warming
her   fingers   there   -- and
    in the warm glow of beleek   -- stroking
the creamer's base   -- imagining
    the local doubts   and   all   that charged
astonishment   -- the looks of kids --
    delivering   water   in   well-country --
and   meals   arriving
    unannounced   -- before   she's called
and   asked   for them   -- meals
    like   one more   form   -- of   being
comfortable. So what if the cops
    she thinks   were   thinking   probably --
and   the boys   she's met   -- since
    there'll be everything to tell   -- striding
in air   -- when   air   had seemed
    impossible   -- were   finding   another
use   for   tools   -- another   use
    for   that folk art   and   local history --
quaint as these quaint kids seem --
    as the sportsboys seem   -- pedalling
their bikes   down   school steps
    toward an adventure   -- and   voices
that might be steer   / be   stars
    over the dark chimneys   -- visiting
again   as trains   and   trains
    of faces visit her*

*

They come with their candies and bread treats --
their desires for her pre-set
    and   all   that   meant   nineteen once --
and   all   that   the tall men
    seemed   -- bending   their tongues
to her   -- their   wills
    to   confiscate   -- and   all
of   this   gliding
    company   -- walking on air
and   following
    the   air's motion
off
    that slope.

*

Tonight   might have   meant so much --
and   this   last light   feathering
    the textured walls and bedcovers   -- this
breathing she thinks she sees
    and   almost   sees appreciate   -- where
trains solidify   -- the carnival motion
    swells   -- in   all that   gliding company --
having agreed to walk   in just such ways
    before the world. And maybe   she's raked
ton-loads. Maybe   she's   thinking
    films   -- thinking   some   street   song
just above a whisper   as   Time glides --
    where nothing   but darkness   sits   -- and
nothing but darkness   -- finished off
    to suit   -- condensed   in   this   room
/ this solitaire   -- where   she has been
    waiting   days   -- arranging   the notes
for relatives   -- explaining   the films

    again   -- and   all   the modest ways
she's suffered   -- given   the week
    spun down   / the grand-daughters
beginning mittens   / or   tearing
    mittens out   -- setting her dreams
on   the hill routes   / on
    the   hill homes   dressed
in   vinyl flowers   and
    false brick.

            *

    So what if she's still their centerfold
/ if all she has dreamed
and   understood   -- spoken
to green stone --
moves   in the light
/ the absence
of light   -- in
accidental
wind?

    She'll let them have their summertimes --
selling that Cessna
    part-by-part there on the front lawn --
piecing the reasons out --
    blowing the dust off calendars --
off letters
    they   might have   sealed
and addressed --
    posted   somewhere
/ any   other
    once.

    She'll let them have their summertimes --
and let them have
    the cast of winters afterward   -- stroking
the creamer's base,
    and   warming   her fingers   there
in   the warm   glow
    of   beleek   -- watching the trucks blow by --
their doubtful fenders
    snagging wind   -- following   the cheer
and   modes   of cheer
    till   her gaze   fails   -- remembering
the breezy   and   local songs --
    here   -- on   the south shoulder --
half-way   to   Alliance --
    and   *here*   -- where   the freeway
ends   in   jiffy-lubes
    and   pit stops   -- a   man
ignoring
    the   clotheslines'   dip --
the downswaying limbs --
    the looks   of this storm
blown-in   / and
    now   this   storm
locked-in   -- from
    all directions
lacking one.

Robert Lietz

Breughel Afterward

    The hunters   / hunters' wives   -- a family's worth of plaids   encircled

    by the pick-ups   -- welcome the night's first stars / the looks of the homes   the families

    dress   with Christmas strands   and porch-bulbs -- considering   what cold   must feel like --

    and love   -- come eye-to-eye   -- more   keenly scaled   -- remembering

    the last   of twelve more hours   freshly spent. Even as   twi-bright   clouds   dissolve   -- and

    the stars   -- like chords   the later cold delivers on -- appear   with   the first stars   then --

    they stand   for the moment   under it   -- there -- as   the sumptuous   attains   -- abstracted

    as hearts composed   -- at the center   of embrace -- without   a ceiling   overhead   -- or

    boards   below   to interfere with. Maybe desire's only   another way   to tell   -- a matter

    of flesh among   -- and   only   their innocence -- and then   -- once   they   have   learned

    to meet   their nature   face to face   -- and once   -- when   they hear

    their voices drop   -- having   learned
themselves   to speak   the stars'

    least whisperings.

Robert Lietz

Wheels

For J.W., M.W.

    The boys will be   trying out the bar --
the cardtables and decks --
    the chairs set round   -- to warm them
for the evening   -- because
    the springtime's full of it   -- the Biscayne's
exciting a few toward memory --
    even that storm-laced scrap   -- defining
the yard around   for decades --
    asking   for open space   -- for once more
on the truck routes. This   morning
    the geese   -- like   graces   -- heads-high
in winter wheat   -- and   the cops
    gradespeed   -- knowing   how the rigs
kick out   and   vanish   after daylight --
    leaving   these   cups   behind   -- these
condoms   and   diapers   -- littering
    the ridge   they've   claimed for seasons --
and how the boys still up   / stiff   from
    another woolen night   spent in the sleepers --
wash down   the longest rides   indoors --
    letting   the morning come   -- arranging
daylight just for them   -- on   something
    like 1956   -- two-toned   in   forest / mint
and fresh as the coming green   -- because
    his hands   have seen to it   -- the only thing
outside   the roadhouse eats   still lively --
    until   this   gothic-scripted   scooped Goat
pulls along beside it   -- hidden for months
    maybe   -- and   as   wide-rubbered   now
as any April urgency. So the spiced eggs
    go down easy   with the longnecks. So some
of the boys cut up   -- and some   -- with
    fifty springs   the evenings class and stratify --
are sure what surveillance means to them --
    what the lavender   and   bone-bad luxury
inspire   -- *bone-bad for heavens' sake!* --

    as if the rich   had   just as many sutures
they could brag on   -- whatever
    the morning   means to them   -- and
the night ahead   -- the card-playing
    to follow   -- the scripture   -- according
to stone   -- and   the moonlight --
    suited   to the music   -- the moon --
according   to   being young
    and seeming keen.

Robert Lietz

Legacy

life becomes insane
when nocturnal demons
chase us thru the dawn

endless cemetery years
buried in adhesive tears
now the Scythe seeks to mesh
with your weak, mind-tortured flesh

child of sorrow,
maiden of sadness,
erect my gallows
in your madness

we leave behind
brilliant shadows of our lives

Rod Walker

Opake

thrust into the sudden trance of eternity

pale goddess, lost daughter,
come with us

we of the swamp's glow
we of the black-robed phantom in the hills
we of the night

choose your fantasies & your life among us
out here there are no chains
we are free from disguise

run with us
we call on you to dance

eclipsed is the view, shadowless the fate

Rod Walker

Search

sandalwood smoke ascends
summoning ancestors
slumbering on slow winds

ghosts of golden centuries & spirits thick as flesh
quicken my pen with revelations
our pale hides conceal

all has been written--
hidden in familiar possibilities
star-wrought testaments burn for us
thru the ancient void

in a new mind,
in a fresh mind's eye,
breathes the bounty of a thousand wounded dreamers

Rod Walker

Hawk Watch at Pranker's Pond

(for John and Ellen Burns)

Up gray stairs cut against the heart of earth,
taller than promise, shade given over
to hail evening's climb and gray-ridden rocks,
we mount to the everlasting station
where your scrutiny lingers on this pond.

When I was a boy I fished these rocks
flushed out of this shore, like a miner's earth
tossed by shovel to make an edge of pond,
here, below you, topography's station,
charred granite edges, time rolling over

from a long-dead fire, Ice Age hunting earth
and plush haven to put down Pranker's Pond,
to slam it meteoric among rocks
as if, in hindsight, no other station
could accept tumbling over and over.

One animate god gave you this pond,
watch guard from Christmas Eve to Passover,
all ends of the track up to the station,
all shore, all watering, and sculptured rocks,
all good ministries of this piece of earth;

where big-mouth bass, and pickerel under rocks,
and carp, gathered in flotilla's station
like dark submarines, lingering at earth,
once lined up in Le Havre, New London's pond,
waiting for silence to come, and over

their grayed and lichened surfaces the pond
accepts what peace comes, absolute station,
accepting, if by chance, peace under rocks
and all the dread world over, all over.
Nothing is so quiet as quiet earth,

nothing comes knifelike between earth and pond
like erosion, misdeeds, molestation
of waters, herbs, young saplings, Mother Earth,
pieces of Saugus, what you watch over
from that aerie on precipitous rocks.

Nothing moves you do not see, slate of pond,
duck, bluebird, cardinal calling out its mirth,
a dozen crows a starched pine gives over
to the fact of day, sad face of storm clocks,
clouds cascading down sweet immolation.

You, un-winged, un-feathered, are the hawks
who give their eyes to long-established bond,
who see seasons, under scan, recover
in part and whole, the essence of rebirth,
a cursed pond come back from profanation.

Tom Sheehan

Saugus, Embassy of the Second Muse

He has come out of a dread silence and given himself a name;
Saugus, he says. He bleats like a tethered goat to come out of that
coming, to be away, dense spiral to the core of self, to the
mountain call, bird arc across such slopes of pale imaginings.
Saugus, he says: I am that part of you cries not for the love but
intimacy of words, light touch of skin we dread and seek, owning
up of self as if in another. I am that part of you named endless
searcher, thirsty one, guzzler, sufferer, warred on, the starved and
the wasted, that part of you you can't turn over by yourself. I
have the
secrets you do not know you know. I am lodged in a far corner of
mind, some fallow place at reins' end, waiting to be routed out,
turned up, to green a page again. Has it taken you so long to find
me, or do you ignore me and try it on your own? You cannot
avoid documented lightning, shock of metaphor, God on one
knee, Saugus. I am not a stranger. I breathe with you, find shelter
and warmth when you do, know the single star haunting the edge
of your horizon, know best of all the magic when
the sound is right, Oh, Thomas! when the sound is the music of
one word upon another, and it tears two parts of soul to four
because nothing like it has been heard before, when the word
dances on its consonants, slides on soft vowels, when the spine
knows the word is known by every ganglia, thong and sinew of
the body. The coring.

I am Saugus and you waste me away, cast me aside. I who carry
all sounds of memory, cast me aside at breast-panning, when you
lose the music down in some phantom crotch, when a sweet ass
ties your brain in knots. Now, just now, Thomas, feel the core
wind in. Feel the word rock in you. Find the word rock. Chip at
it. Let the chisel fly, the sparks dance out globally, the word
broken away from the granite source in you. Don't you know me,
Thomas? I am the gate tender. I am the one who lets you find the
word rock. I am the keyman. I let you into that vast field of
yourself where the rock grows. I am Saugus, and I tend that field
where the rock lies in the sacred cairn. We meet so infrequently. I
keep myself here waiting on you, the gate eager to rise, the field
waiting to know your tread, the rock waiting to be beat upon by

the hammer of your desire. I am lonely when you wander. It is dark and fearful without you. And yet I can make you cry when I am lonely. You don't believe me yet... I am Saugus who makes you cry.

You can't tease me, please me, appease me. Just use me. I am servant of servants. I am Id's Id's Id, ego sans ego sans ego. I am to be used, exploited, submitted. And I guard that huge rock in you, tend it, know what filled it dense as hardpan that time in Boxford field and you hurt all over; dense as the frozen earth DeMatteo dug fox holes with C-3 and it finally blew off the back of his head and Colonel Mason said, "Shit!"; dense as Vinegar Hill or Indian Rock or that rock wall outside Schenectady and you stopped to change a tire at her waving and she slid down that wall at her back motioning to you her bodily gratitude. Dense is that word rock, full of all your lore and legend bricked with every movement you've ever known, all sights and sounds and music of the words; that special place where the thing rings in you, that place of core vibration.

Jesus, Thomas, take my hand again! Walk in the field with me. We belong together, you and I. Dispel me of doom. Let the music of words come, let them dance first in your eye, roll on your tongue, live to die on the page. Let them vibrate on your spine, get kissed of your skin, shoot out of here in flight of geese, and mournful sound of heading home when there is no home, steaming freight train whistle calling you from a circle of blue nights, self shout at the moon still shining on a hill East of Cleveland, South of Yang-du, East again a long stretch from the Chugach given you in a word picture, West of a cliff near Kerry and rain moved as a god laughing at the rootstock of your silence, Celtic mummery, God buried in stone. If you can't come with me, Thomas, you are the loser, lonely, forsaken. I can take you back to all the hard places, to the adjectives and verb ends; to the quadrangle in Japan in 1951 and the cool wind coming through Camp Drake and the voice of death talking in it and calling out all your comrades' names and it didn't talk your name and you still felt sad and knew you were the only ear. In three weeks they were gone, all gone, and their voices went into ground, and all their words, and they built on the word rock and now they still dance sadly… such words that make you cry with music still in them, and they come long and slowly out of another time funnel, like Billy Pigg cursing as he rolled over in your arms and Captain Kay saying, "I just want to go home to Memphis for a little while and tell Merle and Andy I love them. Just for an hour or so."

Ah, Thomas, come home again. Come home again.

Tom Sheehan

"Land Shark!"

I am the master
of whatever happens.
No worries

about death by stingray,
as I quash every opportunity
for murder

or maiming at sea.
I own my destiny
as I don't

even venture into
Lake Michigan,
for fear a

fresh-water stingray
might seek me out,
to kill me.

William Hicks

I'm Okay

Sorry for the delay.
I can only say
it stinks when I write.
And it stinks when I don't.
It seems like
a chore to communicate.
I know you'd
like to know
how it's going
with my new job.
So would I.

Let's just say
I've been
a little "constipated."
Mentally.
I can't think.
I can't write.
If I were home
I'd tell you
About my torn cuticle
and mental Exlax.
Not now.

Things are different, here
I'm different, here.
Okay, so maybe
Springfield, Illinois
isn't great.
It's no Chicago.
But it is someplace, else.
Someplace other than
Rogers Falls, Indiana.
The little hole
where you live,
and I used to,
is downright small.

I'm getting
big in the head.
Six months
 and I'm getting
big in the head.
I promised
I'd never do that.
Yet, now I'm doing just that.
Sorry—I mean it sincerely.

It's just I expected
more.
Something special.
And nothing special
ever happens in Rogers Falls.
Don't cry.
You're special.
You happened.
That's why we
get along so well.

I know you understand.
You always do.
Isn't that odd:
I know 25 people.
But you're the one
who understands.
The only person
I can speak with.
As the saying goes,
I'm okay.
You're okay.
We're all okay.
Or is it …

I scream,
you scream,
we all…"

William Hicks

Beeeep

"Hallo."
"Hello? Who is this?"
 My name's Sally."
"You're not who I called."
"You were just
leaving a message
 on my machine."

"Oh, I'm so sorry.
Please erase it.
I misdialed.
I was leaving myself
a reminder call.
Please, please,
don't listen.
Just erase it.
Thank you
and have
a good day."

William Hicks

Inwood Indiana

Inwood Indiana

Made in the USA
Charleston, SC
28 July 2011